Bench Buddies

Humor, Philosophy, and Tales from the Educational Trenches and the Neighborhood Benches

By Chuck Sodergren

PublishAmerica
Baltimore

First printing

At the specific preference of the author, PublishAmerica allowed this work to remain exactly as the author intended, verbatim, without editorial input.

ISBN: 1-4241-4585-6
PUBLISHED BY PUBLISHAMERICA, LLLP
www.publishamerica.com
Baltimore

Printed in the United States of America

Dedicated to

Myra, my beautiful wife and the love of my life
for over fifty years

My four children and their spouses; Rick and Janice
Greenlee, Curt and Jane Lewis, Steve and Jenny Sodergren,
and Bob and Janeen Horton

My ten grandchildren;
Brett, Erin, Heather, Brooke, Breanna, Sydney, Audrey,
Trey, Joey, and Andie

Barbara Apps, my supportive and caring big sister

My current and past Friday morning breakfast buddies
and the memory of my Friday afternoon coffee buddies at
The Pad

The COBRA travel group

My Heroes—Harold Hypse and Bernie Johnson

All of my former teammates in the Education profession

My fellow Optimists

And the pastor and members of Trinity Lutheran Church,
Topeka, Kansas

Contents

Introduction

There are at least several hundred people alive today from all parts of the world, mostly older males, who sometime in the past for one short 15 to 30 minute period functioned as my *bench buddy*. My relationships with these bench buddies were close, personal, and very intense, but also very short-lived. The only thing that we had in common was that we shared a bench, or seat of some kind, while we rested at a shopping mall, park, or department store or while we rode on the same airplane, bus, or train. Usually, but not always, both of us had a wife or family that would soon meet us while we were just killing time and resting. Our conversation usually started with some cliché about the weather, sports, how old age is catching up with us, or some reference to how things just are not what they used to be in the good old days. Before we would go our separate ways, never to see each other again, we would share stories and even talk about personal things that we would be embarrassed to talk about to people we must face every day. Each of these bench buddies added one drop into my bucket of happiness that, over a lifetime, has filled to overflowing.

Fortunately, I also have many long-term bench buddies.

These are my closest friends. We love to sit, usually sipping a fresh cup of coffee, and share stories. We practice the philosophy that coffee, like life, should be consumed slow and easy. We want to enjoy the taste and flavor of both coffee and life and relish the experience. Every community and small town has a supply of old codgers and bright young whippersnappers sitting on benches expounding wit, wisdom, and comic stories with exaggerated humor.

We sit so much that our pants wear out on the rear ends. We suffer from a disease that an old Swedish man in jest called "Soreasses." We engage in Creative Loitering. When we move we stroll, amble, mosey, meander, wander, saunter, and dawdle.

The word *Loiter* has been the victim of bad public relations. It is usually used with the word *No* as in *No Loitering*, or with the word *Soliciting* as in *No Loitering or Soliciting*. One is led to believe that loitering is a negative activity, and that loiterers are bad people. I have always thought this might be unfair. After considerable deliberation about this situation, I decided to consult the dictionary. Loiter is defined as, *"To spend time idly; to linger, dawdle; to walk or move slowly with frequent stops and pauses along the way."* Wow! I can't see anything wrong with that! To the contrary, most people would be better off if they loitered more. Everyone should linger awhile, relax, go with the flow, walk slowly, dilly-dally, and stop to smell the roses along the way. We could benefit by spending more time sitting on the front porch cleaning our eye glasses so we get a clearer image of reality, and converting our bathrooms into a library annex. We need to devote more time to the important Three R's; of Rememberin', Reflectin', and Reminiscin'. Since I retired I have spent most of my time loitering, and I don't feel like it has been time wasted. Signs should be put up around the community that say, "PLEASE LOITER HERE." The best things in life move slowly. We are making haste to ill purpose if we haven't taken time to read good books, to think quietly, to visit our friends, to comfort the sick and sorrowing, to enjoy the beautiful creations of God and man, and to lend a hand to a struggling brother. We need to slow down and live one day at a time. A religious leader suggested that a good way to nourish your whole self, body and soul as one, is to be quiet, sit still, and listen to your deepest self, your soul. I call that loafing.

We should form a club called the, "Spit-and-whittle spinners of tall-tales on Main Street." The rural version could be a "Loafer's and Liar's Club that meets to Gossip on the South Side of Barns in the Winter." We must avoid becoming a group that some might call the "Croakers, Grumblers, and Fretters."

I am by nature a saver and collector. My garage and basement are my archive rooms. They are cluttered with old buckets, funeral and wedding notices, and family heirlooms that I have collected from various sources. The most important things that I have collected are the written records of the many events that have occurred and the stories that I have heard. Many of the stories and ideas shared here came from my bench buddies and fellow creative loiterers. My interests are usually not terribly academic. The commonplace and daily aspects of life attract me most, and the anecdotal essay is my style of reporting what I notice. I prefer the informal, backstage view of life. It is always gratifying to see something familiar in a new light, and to realize that what I'm looking for is close by. It's like finding my "lost" glasses perched on the end of my nose. And most of all, it's fun!

Social life for retirees consists of going to the supermarket, filling our baskets half-way, and standing around talking to anyone who might come by. We can usually count on knowing at least half of the other shoppers. We enjoy clipping coupons out of the newspaper, comparing prices, and buying products that are on "Special." I make sure I don't miss any of the samples they are giving out. I have sampled chocolate cake, seafood, cheese, chicken, macaroni, cranberry juice, beef, French fries, cookies, and candy. On one occasion I made the mistake of filling my mouth up with what I thought was a sample of divinity candy that was in reality lye soap. I might have saved money if I had just bought breakfast instead of the medicine it took to treat my upset stomach, but I had fun and it was worth the trouble because I had a great story to tell!

Let's take it nice and easy. I agree with former president George Bush who said, "What's wrong with being a boring kind of guy?" Some things just can't be hurried—like taking a nap, soaking in the bathtub, and enjoying a beautiful view.

Chapter One
Bench Buddies in the Educational Trenches

The Elementary School Winter Program— One of the major sources of stress for elementary school music teachers is the high priority that they feel the community places on directing a major production at Christmas time and again later in the spring. Christmas programs, which at one time centered around the birth of Jesus Christ, are now called "Winter Programs" and the content now features Santa Claus, snowmen, and reindeer. Although the content has changed, many elementary music teachers continue to feel the need to produce a huge winter extravaganza.

I shared a bench with a retired music teacher while waiting for a musical show to start. She told me that she had little trouble in developing material for the smaller children. They can do almost anything and the audience, especially their parents, will think it is cute. Finding material for the older children, especially boys, that they will do with enthusiasm is a challenge. One year she thought she had finally come up with the perfect solution. The science teacher had been teaching a unit on sound. The two teachers worked as a team to create the different notes of the scale by blowing on pop bottles filled with various amounts of water. The older boys were excited about doing this. The music teacher formed a pop bottle chorus, made up of thirty-five boys. They would play several Christmas carols. Five boys were assigned to each note on the scale. She directed them by pointing to them when they should blow over the top of the bottle. The boys did a tremendous job on the night of the performance, and the curtain came down. The audience let it be known, by their loud and long applause, that they wanted an encore. The two teachers were excited and happy about the obvious success and decided to pull the curtain up and have the boys play "Silent Night" again. This time it sounded terrible! The music teacher explained it this way, "Those little rascals thought that they were done for the evening and drank some of the water out of the bottles because they were thirsty." The audience had a good laugh.

County Champs— A female bench buddy was a teacher in a one room school in Atchison county in 1945. Her basketball team played for the county championship. The team consisted of four boys, and one tall and very well developed girl. The girl was so aggressive that occasionally she would even grab the ball from one of her lethargic teammates. She was the best player on the team, but she didn't own a bra and was embarrassed to play in the championship game wearing the team's T-shirt. The teacher went to the restroom, took off her bra, and loaned it to the girl. They won the championship trophy. The girl scored 30 points and was "high point man." One of the boys was standing at the free throw line waiting to shoot the deciding point when his mother stood up and yelled, "Leroy, if you ever do anything for me, do it now!" He made the shot!

Against the Flow Walkers— My wife and I try to walk two miles every day for exercise. We walk outside when the weather allows, but during bad weather, we walk at the mall. We are joined there by hundreds of other walkers; all circling in a counter-clockwise manner. All, that is, except for one old couple, who are determined to walk clockwise. The old man has a grim look of determination on his face and never looks anyone that he meets in the eye. The old lady hangs onto the old man's arm and looks straight ahead. They plod along; determined, stubborn, resolute, inflexible, and rigid. All of the other walkers wonder why. They don't seem to enjoy playing the role of "Wrong-way Corrigan." I wondered if maybe they might be from England, where you drive cars on the left side of the street; or maybe from south of the equator, where water swirls down drains differently than it does here. Or, someplace in the world where track meets and car races are run clockwise around the track. I found out that the old man's name is Leroy. He is a Democrat, and has vowed to walk against the flow because the Republicans took over Congress during the last election. Now that makes sense! I wonder if he ever played basketball in Atchison county.

The Presentation— I love to wander around in flea markets and thrift stores to see if I can pick up bargains. I once bought a bargain typewriter that had no "A" key and a lamp that my wife had previously donated to that same thrift store. On another occasion, I just couldn't resist buying a very large painting of a mountain scene. It was beautiful and sold for only three dollars. I have done this same thing so many times in the past that I don't have any more room on the walls in my basement or garage. I tried to give it away, but none of my friends shared my enthusiasm for it. The fact that it measured three feet by six feet made it too large to be easily stored away in my backyard shed. I came up with the perfect solution. My wife and I were invited to a party at a fellow teacher's home that evening. I decided that if I couldn't give it away, I could present it to my buddy as a token of the community's appreciation for all that he had done over the many years. I made a public presentation in front of a large group of people. I even made up a story about money being donated by an adoring group of friends and former students. He couldn't turn down such a nice gesture, but the next time I visited his house I didn't see it hanging on any of the walls. It seems he had presented it to another one of our friends. This picture relay could go on forever.

The Stripper— Our female physical education teacher/ coach is a tremendous person and a dedicated, skilled, and experienced educator. She also has a great sense of humor. She once sent a student to get me to come to the gym. When I got there she showed me her chain necklace, which had her keys and whistle on it, hanging down from the rafters. She explained that she was throwing them to her student aide when they got stuck on her fingers and went sailing high into the air and got stuck. Solving that kind of problem was a pleasant break from dealing with student discipline situations and serious injuries that teachers usually send a student to get me to help with. One day she was leaving the building after a long day of teaching and coaching the basketball team. She stayed late to make sure that all of her team members had a ride home. Everyone had finally left the building except the night custodian. She carried some papers out to her car and then remembered something else that she needed to take home. She opened the school door, propped it open with a piece of wood, and left her keys in her car. When she returned and was shutting the door, it blew shut and part of her skirt got stuck in the door. The door was locked and the key was in her car! The night custodian was in the far end of the building and didn't hear her knocking. She wondered out loud, "What can I do?" It was late and cold outside. She couldn't just wait for someone to come along and rescue her. She finally decided that the only solution would be to take her skirt off. She ran the risk that someone would see her in this embarrassing condition, but that was her only option. She undressed right out in front of the school and ran to her car to get the door key. Being the beautiful lady that she is, she had a good laugh before heading home and willingly shared the great story with friends the next day.

Cocaine— I had driven the same route to school for years. One morning, when I was only one block away from the school, I neglected to use my turn indicator when I made a right turn. I was startled to hear a siren. I looked in my rear view mirror and saw red lights blinking. I had no idea what was happening so I pulled over to the side of the road. A big policeman walked up to my open window and politely told me that I had turned without signaling. Then I saw a serious look flash suddenly on his face! His eyes were locked on a plastic bag filled with white powder which was on the seat next to me. I wondered why. Then he asked me to hand it over. I obeyed his request and it suddenly hit me that he must have thought that the white powder was cocaine. I quickly explained that I was attempting to lose weight and that the powder was Ultra Slim that I planned to mix in milk and drink instead of eating lunch. I was thinking that he probably would never believe me, and what a terrible mess I was in, when he said to me, "That explains it, Mr. Sodergren, have a good day." The policeman was a former student! He hadn't recognized me at first, and I sure didn't recognize him. For some strange reason, he seemed to enjoy giving me a ticket. We had a good laugh and he told me he could hardly wait to get back to the station to share this story. Several days later I even saw some humor in the experience.

One Room School Teacher— Back in the days of the one room school house, prospective teachers had to travel to each of three school board members' homes to interview. One former teacher told me that she was in the process of suffering through this ordeal when a storm came up. She ran all over the barnyard helping the farmer catch his chickens. The farmer told her, "Anyone who will help me catch my chickens gets my vote." One of the other board members told her that he had just completed interviewing an applicant who was "Weak in the basics—she couldn't tell me how many pounds a bushel of ear corn weighed." My bench buddy knew how much a bushel of shelled corn weighed, and how much a bushel of wheat weighed, but not an ear of corn. She talked around the subject, and got the farmer's vote; plus an eight month contract at $75 a month. She laughed when she told about an incident that happened on Halloween that year. One old gentleman, named Bus Anderson, had come dressed as a woman for many years. A group of men were visiting outside when in walked an ugly old witch, who just nodded and went in to sit down. They all knew that it was Bus, so one of the men went in the school house, put his arms around the witch and gave her a hug and a pinch, and walked back out. Then, who should walk up but

Bus! He was not in costume this year because he was going to attend a meeting. The man's face was bright red when he realized that he had hugged and pinched his new neighbor's wife; and she was not in costume! He had heard about her but had never met her—until now. First impressions are very important and he was off to a terrible start!

Two Left Feet— I went to the meeting of the Kansas Retired Teacher's Association in June of 2001 in Hutchinson. As we were about to pull out of the garage to leave, Myra asked, "Did you remember to bring your new black dress shoes and your suit coat and tie?" I was shocked that one of us hadn't thought to pack these things. I told her to remain in the car while I ran upstairs to get them. We arrived in Hutchinson and were dressing to attend the first general session, when I discovered I had grabbed two left shoes. Until recently I never had the luxury of owning two pairs of black dress shoes, so I assumed that any two black shoes would be a pair. I wore the old left shoe on my right foot for the remainder of the convention. (It is more broken in than the new one) Myra laughed every time she looked at my feet. I had a great time sharing the experience with my friends from Topeka, and hoped that others wouldn't notice my "two left feet." One of my buddies at the convention told about the time when an old man accidentally walked into the ladies restroom and went into one of the stalls to relieve himself. Later, a lady in the stall next to his said, "I knew something was wrong because the feet were faced the wrong way."

No Sympathy— I earned bachelors and masters degrees in education and worked for thirty-eight years in that field, all but five of those years as a building administrator. I retired over ten years ago. Since that time I have kept busy doing volunteer work. This morning I was working with a buddy, who is the retired owner of a construction business, scraping out the weeds that had grown up in the cracks in the pavement on the sidewalks of the business section of North Kansas Avenue. We were using a large pick, shovels, rakes, and brooms. It was hard work and the weather was very hot and humid. A well dressed old lady came walking along on her way to the beauty shop. I stopped working, and looked up at her with sweat dripping from my entire body, and said with a smile, "It is almost too hot to do hard work like this today." She looked at me with disgust and replied, "You get no sympathy from me. If you had stayed in school and received a good education, you could have a job inside where it is air-conditioned!!" Then she handed me some money and said sarcastically, "Here, use this money to buy yourself some deodorant." Without thinking, I accepted the money. She walked on by, and I continued my work. It caused me to think! She must have thought that I was an old bum, who had squandered away his educational opportunities; and that the Rescue Mission required me to do manual labor in return for food and a place to sleep. It was an inconsiderate comment to make to me, but it would have even been worse if it had been made to someone who hadn't gone to school. I wondered what religious group promoted that style of charity. I had not only used deodorant that morning, but it was the "Official deodorant of the National Basketball Association." What better recommendation can a deodorant have? It was hot, so I quit working. I decided to use the money that the lady had given me to buy a cup of senior discount coffee.

Rusty Old Red Truck— I attended a meeting of retired educators at the Kansas NEA building across the street from Topeka High School. I drove my old, 1984, rusted-out red truck. My truck and I share several characteristics; we are both old and don't sound or look good, but we just keep on chugging along. When I parked in the association parking lot I noticed that there were signs all around warning that unauthorized cars would be ticketed. I was worried that the security man might think it was a high school student's truck and give me a parking ticket for parking there. When I went into the building, I said to the security man, "I parked my truck out in the lot. You won't give me a ticket, will you?" He replied, "Gosh, no, Chuck. I know that's your truck. No high school kid would be caught dead driving it."

An old drunk must have liked the old truck though. I attended a meeting downtown one evening and came out to get in the truck to drive home. I looked in the rearview mirror and noticed that the old drunk had crawled into the bed of my truck and gone to sleep. I shook him and told him he must get out. He said that he was tired and would get out in the morning when he woke up. I didn't like the thought of a drunk waking up in my garage. I considered driving straight to the police station but instead I went back into the meeting and got some help removing him.

Sheriff Badges—The theme park "Silver Dollar City" sells official looking sheriff badges for kids to wear when they play. One of my principal friends wore one of these play badges when he went out rounding up truants. He said that he got great respect and wonderful results! Simple but effective.

Poor Choice of Words—The dad of a boy who had his leg cut off the past summer in an accident demanded that the boy be provided a special bus to get him to school. He said he was getting a lawyer and going to court. I said, "Go ahead, you don't have a leg to stand on." That was a poor choice of words, just as it was when I complained at a meeting about our head cook's "soggy buns." I apologized later.

Stool Samples—For over twenty years I sat on the same old worn out stool when I supervised students in the school commons area. One day my much beloved stool was missing. I got on the PA system and appealed to whoever had taken the stool to return it. A group of intelligent and creative students thought they would have some fun over the incident. They told me over the intercom that they might buy me a new stool. They asked me "Do you want us to send some STOOL SAMPLES to the office?" I caught on to their idea of humor right away. The missing stool mysteriously showed up the next day.

They Never Forget—The teacher in a one room school house during the 1920s asked Billy Crim, "Which is more important, the moon or the sun?" Billy thought for a while and replied, "The moon." The teacher was upset and said, "Why do you think that?" Billy answered matter-of-factly, "The moon shines at night when we need light, the sun shines in the daytime when we don't need light." All of the students laughed loudly. Billy was called "Moon Crim" from that day on. His obituary seventy years later even referred to him as William "Moon" Crim.

McDonald's—A sixth grade teacher threatened one of her students, "Do your homework or you will end up working at McDonald's." Later in the day she had a conference with the boy's mom and was told that the boy's goal in life is to someday work at McDonald's. Speaking of McDonald's, a friend of mine was on a trip up in Minnesota when he came to a town with a long hard-to-pronounce Native American name. He decided to call his parents to tell them where he was and how long it would be before he joined them. He stopped at a fast food chain and asked a worker there, "How do you pronounce where I'm at?" The worker said, "McDonald's!"

Misunderstanding—A mother and her two sons approached the ticket taker at a basketball game. A sign on the wall read, "Children below school age are free." The ticket taker said to the pre-school aged child, "You don't need to pay, you are free." The child, thinking that he wasn't going to be allowed to go into the game, became visibly upset and replied loudly, "Oh, no, I am not free, I'm four!"

Stuck on Spot—One of my older bench buddies attended a one room school when he was young. He told me about one of his male friends, who was large for his age but not very smart. He was supposed to be in the fourth grade, but had trouble reading so the teacher kept him in the first grade reading book. When school started one year, he opened up his reading book, and looked up and said, "Oh (*expletive deleted*) not Spot again!"

This same guy said that he experienced his first serious romantic encounter when he was only 14 with a mature girl of 21. When it got hot and heavy, she had an epileptic seizure and at first he thought he had really turned her on.

No Worries—When I was a Jr. High principal I looked forward to going to meetings at the Central Office building. It was great to be able to get a drink from a drinking fountain without first having to check to see if there is gum in it, and whether it had been tampered with so it would squirt water into my eyes.

The Pool Hall—I came out of a downtown restaurant and I observed a young lady struggling along carrying a crying baby and pushing a young child in a stroller. It was a bitterly cold and windy day. I thought that she really had her hands full with two children to worry about in such terrible weather. As we got nearer to each other, I recognized the lady as a girl that had attended the Jr. High where I had been principal. As a student she had been in constant trouble. I had suspended her from school on multiple occasions. I wondered if she would recognize me and, worse yet, if she continued to harbor unpleasant feelings towards me. I gave her a cheerful "Hello" and she immediately acknowledged me in a very pleasant manner. She even surprised me by saying that I was her favorite teacher! She was headed for a city bus stop several blocks away. She was going to the emergency department of the hospital to get her baby some medicine for his pneumonia. I took pity on her and offered to drive her and the kids to the hospital in my truck. We put the stroller in the bed of the truck and the four of us crowded into the cab. On the way to the hospital, she told me all of her troubles while the kids screamed and kicked, and practically destroyed the interior of the truck and the dashboard. She yelled loudly at them but had no control over them. We finally arrived at our destination and I breathed a sigh of relief as I watched them struggle toward the hospital door. Then she suddenly turned around and came back to the truck. In her hand she had a white pool ball. She handed it to me and said, "Before I met you we went into the pool hall to warm up and so I could drink a beer. Bobby played with the balls on the pool table and I just noticed that he took the cue ball with him. Please return the ball to them. They are probably really mad about this." She handed me the pool ball, and before I could think of a way to refuse her request, she was out of sight. That particular beer joint had a very bad reputation. Two killings had occurred there in the past year; and both killings involved arguments about a game of pool. They take the game of pool very seriously! I had allowed myself to get into a no-win situation. If I didn't return the pool ball, she would tell them that I had it. If I did return it they would assume that I had taken it. They sure wouldn't treat the guy who had stolen their cue ball kindly. I walked into the dark bar, explained as best that I could what had happened, and waited for the consequences. A group of mean looking guys came forward, took a long look at me, and said, "Thanks a lot Mr. Sodergren. It's nice to see you again. How's it going?" Then I recognized them as kids that I had in school years ago. We celebrated a grand reunion! They said that all that they are today they owe to me! I breathed a sigh of relief and moved on.

The Bragger—One old man stood up at a meeting and said proudly, "I've been coming to these meetings as long as I can remember!" His wife, who was sitting next to him, yelled out, "Yes, but he can only remember what happened back to about 15 minutes ago." He thinks that she is anxious for him to die so she can collect the insurance money. His evidence … "She feeds me lots of greasy eggs every morning."

Six-Trait Writing— We were all excited and proud a year ago when the writing test results came back from the state raters. Our best male basketball player, who we had not previously looked upon as being a gifted writer, was rated very high in all of the categories of the six-trait writing model except the more traditional ones like punctuation and spelling. The judges were impressed by his organization, content, originality, and what they call voice. Recently one of our teachers read his composition to her class as an example of an excellent paper. One of the students recognized it as a popular rap piece. The next day he brought a copy of the tape to school. Sure enough, there was our newly discovered genius' composition on tape for all to hear. The funny thing was that for one whole year we had looked at the young man as being intellectually gifted and he had actually responded very positively. We learned three things from the experience: (1) People who judge young people's writing better be familiar with the literature of the streets; if the young man had plagiarized from William Shakespeare he would have been discovered immediately, (2) How you perceive a person has a great effect on how you treat him, and (3) The raters actually liked a type of literature that they had previously put down as being inferior. It was like finding out that you like some kind of food when you accidentally eat it. Our dethroned writing genius won the discus competition at the big league track meet. I told him, "Now that you are good at discussing, you should move up to the next level of competition, which is debate." For some reason nobody but me thought this comment was funny.

Suggestion Box—The following input was given by student bench buddies in the "Suggestion Box" in the school commons:
(1) Cancel the "Assertiveness Training" PTA program for the group of parents that confronted the Board of Education about overcrowding in Kindergarten. They don't need it!
(2) Call our double elimination wrestling tournament the "Diarrhea Tournament."
(3) Have a "Double Gifted" class for those who are very smart.
(4) We could improve our school secretaries' morale by giving them the flowers that are left over from funerals or get flowers from the cemeteries after Memorial Day to give them.
(5) Put beepers on hearing aids so the deaf can find them and buy some solar powered flashlights.
(6) Put a weight limit on cheerleaders.
(7) Get a ZIP machine to put a little zip in our lives.

Withheld Final Grades— Dr. Leon Woods had been a professor of Economics at a major university in the mid-west for nearly forty years. He was so completely immersed in the study of Economic philosophy that he never married and had no interest in other matters. His students affectionately referred to him as "Foggy Woods" because he always appeared to be in a mental fog. He was the classic absentminded professor. He always placed his pocket watch on his desk so he would know how much time remained in the period. On the last day of school he noticed that his watch was missing. Perhaps it had been stolen as a harmless prank, or worse yet, maybe it was just plain thievery. He announced that he would not release any final grades in that class until his watch was returned. Most of his students were seniors and needed the class credit to graduate and begin their job search. A group of them went to the Dean of the Department of Economics and asked him to intervene. The Dean was sympathetic but said that there was little that he could do because Professor Woods was very highly respected and tenured. He suggested that they should check with the jeweler who had worked on Dr. Wood's watch for many years. It was possible that he had taken the watch in to be repaired and forgotten about it. The group of students checked with the jeweler, but to no avail. He did, however, suggest a possible solution to their problem. He said that a down-and-out cowboy had recently passed through town and offered to sell him a watch that was identical to the one owned by Dr. Woods. He told the cowboy that he didn't buy watches and directed him to the corner pawn shop. The cowboy may have pawned the watch. If he had, they could take up a collection, buy the watch, and give it to Dr. Woods so he would release their grades. Everything worked out as planned. The students reluctantly took up a collection and went to Dr. Woods and presented him with the watch. He was happy and said that he had known all of the time that the guilty party would eventually give up the watch if enough pressure was put on him by the group. He reached down to the lower drawer of his desk and unlocked it to get the valuable final test results and grades. There, just where he had put it for safe keeping, was his much sought after watch. Being a gentleman, Professor Woods paid them the value of the second watch, swallowed his pride, and apologized. He even wrote a public apology in the student newspaper and signed it, "Professor Foggy Woods."

Rock Club—In any school one can find students who are not well accepted by others, are considered strange, and who need attention and tender loving care. The *"Rock Club"* was formed to meet the needs of some of these students. Members never knew whether the club studied rocks or rock music. It really never mattered, because just belonging to a group, where they were accepted and could express opinions, was the important thing. Everyone was an officer. All grade levels had a separate president, vice-president, program chairman, sergeant-in-arms, parliamentarian, secretary, treasurer, etc. The club met each week in the principal's office. All of the meeting time was devoted to reading the minutes of the last meeting, reciting a code of ethics in unison, discussing, and other bureaucratic endeavors. The "Rock Club" got credit for sponsoring everything that was done in the school that was not sponsored by some other group. The club met a deep need for its members—to be accepted. Rock Club alumni keep in contact and are a close knit group. They meet regularly to talk about the good old days.

Chapter Two
Conversations on Community Benches

Friday Afternoon Coffee Buddies—For over twenty years, eight of us older guys had a standing appointment every Friday afternoon for a coffee drinking and problem solving group at "The Pad" restaurant. Among us we had experienced almost every physical problem imaginable, including cancer. We joked that we all must stay alive because our buddies are in no shape to serve as pallbearers. Over the years we discussed such high level topics as "The history of lawnmowers in my family," "Runaway dogs," "Cars we have owned over the years," "Confrontations with snakes," "The time I won playing BINGO," and "Is there one official groundhog or lots of them that we need to watch on Groundhog day." We have discussed the relative merits of the quality of toilet paper at various fast food chains, and whether to start a petition to get a symbol for public restrooms on all city maps so us old guys can find one when we need it. One of the guys started every sentence with

"And anyway;" one ended everything he says with, "One thing and another," and another repeatedly said, "On the other hand." I, of course, have no idiosyncrasies like that! We taped a dollar bill under the table top, with the understanding that the last one alive got to keep it.

All of these guys, except me, have died and I do not find these vanishing acts at all amusing! I am tired of preparing eulogies and attending funerals. I'm worried about having anyone left to be pallbearers at my own funeral. But—I got the dollar bill!

My Friday coffee buddy, Duane, would have been 85 years old later that year. He grew up on a farm and early in his adulthood he worked as a farmhand. He and his wife Polly had managed a roller skating rink in a small town back in the 1940s where he skated every day. He could skate backwards and could even do twirls. He went on to farm and be the head custodian at our high school. He hadn't skated for over 50 years, except for the time about 20 years ago when he accompanied his grandson's 4-H group on a club roller skating party. On that occasion he had acted like he couldn't skate. He fell down on purpose and hung on to the side bar like a complete novice. The kids said they would hold him up and teach him how to skate. He wobbled along for a short time and then, much to everyone's surprise, he sailed away from them and showed his stuff. Everyone cheered and laughed. He told the guys in our coffee group about the incident, and we challenged him to skate one more time. We made plans to meet at a local rink where we could drink coffee while Duane roller skated. Before we could get this organized, the unexpected happened!

Polly, Duane's wife of over 65 years, died unexpectedly and, as one would expect, he took it hard. He had been taking chemo-therapy to treat his cancer for the past several years, and

27

expected that he would die before Polly. He had sold the camper-trailer, in which the two of them had enjoyed so many enjoyable trips, so that she wouldn't be bothered with making decisions about how to sell it after he was no longer there to help her. He had serious difficulty getting any sleep for weeks after her death. He even skipped our Friday coffee group twice.

Polly had always made clam chowder soup on Christmas Eve for Duane and his two sons and a daughter. Duane thought he would carry on that tradition. He went to several stores to get the best bargain, and finally bought eight cans of clam chowder. He took them home and mixed all eight cans in a large pot with other stuff that he remembered Polly putting in. While the soup was cooking on the stove he decided to take the trash outside. He put both hands in the trash can to push it down to compact it. In doing so, he hit the sharp edge on the lid of a soup can and suffered a deep cut on one of his fingers. Because of the medicine he was taking as part of his chemo-therapy treatment, his blood was thin and he had a very difficult time getting the bleeding to stop. At last the bleeding slowed down, and the soup was cooked. He was now ready to take the sacred soup over to his daughter's home to share with his family. He put on his coat, carefully picked up the soup, and carried it out to the car. He had to get the keys out of his pocket, so he set the soup down on the hood of the car. Then it happened! The soup kettle slid and all of the soup poured out on the ground. He felt that life couldn't get any worse! He just sat there and stared blankly out into space. Tears welled up in his eyes when he told us about it; a condition we all shared.

We convinced Duane to come back to our group by telling him that we needed him. The first time he came back for coffee he was very embarrassed when he started to cry in front of us. We told him that we understood, and one of the guys even convinced him to go to a music concert with him that night. After a few weeks, he was more like his old self; reciting poems that he had learned in grade school and telling stories. He told us that he didn't think he could have made it without the help of his "Support Group." We were all surprised to hear that. We had all stayed in close contact with him and had no idea that he had been seeing a psychiatrist for group therapy. Then he explained it to us; "I haven't seen a psychiatrist, you guys are all I needed. You are my support group! I couldn't have made it without you. Thanks!" All of us about fainted. We had no idea that we were anything more than a bunch old men drinking coffee and visiting with our good buddies.

I learned that we are all part of a multitude of "Support Groups"— family, friends, civic club members, co-workers, the "fellowship of believers at our church," and even old men drinking coffee. It helps to consciously recognize these groups as our "Support Groups," and do our part to make them effective.

When we are not in a group, we can be "Support Individuals."

Duane suffered in the hospital for several weeks. Then he was transferred to the Hospice, where he slowly faded away and died. During the last week of his life his support group visited him everyday. Duane was ready to rejoin the majority of our coffee group in heaven. I can look forward to doing the same someday. But I'm not in any hurry! In my mind's eye, I can see him now enjoying clam chowder soup that doesn't spill with Polly, telling stories to his old buddies, and roller skating effortlessly and painlessly around the Heavenly Skating Rink.

Relaxing on a Bench— I was holding my baby grandson when two old ladies came up and said, "Hi there, cutie, you're so sweet I would like to take you home with me!" I was shocked until I realized that they were referring to my grandson, not me. Another time I dozed off while sitting on a bench. I had been drinking coffee and held the empty cup on my lap. Some nice lady walked up and put a nickel in the cup.

It reminded me of the time when one of my bench buddies volunteered at a Rotary Club meeting to ring the bell for the Salvation Army. A lady put money in the pot and also handed my buddy two dollars and told him "Get yourself something to eat." A bench buddy bragged, "I can do anything I set my mind to do, if I can only keep awake." The same know-it-all claimed that he had invented manure and that he could remember things that happened before he was born. He complained that his wife celebrated her own birthday for three days, and made a specially decorated cake for the dog on its birthday, but never even gave him a card on his birthday. She refused to allow him to get more than one month's quantity of prescription drugs because she thought he might die any time and it would be a terrible waste of money. Also, she wouldn't allow him to get a much needed pacemaker for his heart because, "You might die and then your heart would keep on beating forever and it would confuse everyone." He and his wife separated and he got the canary and she got the dog. He was proud that he had outsmarted her because "Now she has to take the dog for a ride in the truck every day." He was worried because he had bought a raffle ticket and hoped he didn't win because he didn't want the prize. He showed me a wall plaque that he had purchased for a quarter at an estate sale. It had the words, "*The World's Greatest Grandpa*" engraved on it. I asked him when he was going to give it to his grandpa. He said that his grandpa has been dead for years and that he bought the plaque for himself. He said, "I'm on a year long Spring Break." Sometimes, when I talk with guys like this I feel like I woke up in the middle of a soap opera. He claimed to be president of the local Hospice Alumni Association. I doubt that because when you graduate from the Hospice you are dead. He looked me straight in the eye and said, "I've had a hard day at the office. I guess I'll walk down to the bench in the next block so I can visit with a higher class bum."

I got up, walked over to a potted plant, and poured my lukewarm coffee in the pot. I hope the caffeine didn't make the plant nervous and cause it to lose sleep. I enjoy eating, so I drag it out as long as I can. I eat 99 cent specials and get senior citizen discount coffee. By going to several different places I am usually successful in finding someone to talk to and to share stories with. I always bring a small bottle so I can take any of my left-over pancake syrup home.

One guy said, "I went on a treasure hunt yesterday." After further inquiry it came out that he had spent the day digging through trash dumpsters. That reminded me of the time, years ago, when my kids took up high jumping. I thought I would help, so I constructed a high jump pit in the backyard. We needed something soft for them to land on, so my buddy and I went to a mattress company and asked if they had any old used mattresses that we might have. They directed us to the dumpster where they discarded unwanted mattresses, and told us to help ourselves. I was inside the dumpster and my buddy was in the bed of his truck next to it, when we looked out at the street and saw the head of our Parent-Teacher Association driving by and waving to us. We waved back, and wondered how we would explain being in that part of town rummaging through a dumpster. We explained it the next day and we all had a big laugh.

I recall seeing "No Rats" written crudely on a public trash can in San Francisco. I wondered if that meant that California rats could read and were being advised that they were not welcome, or maybe that bums could rummage through that can without fear because no rats were in it.

Another old bum said that his nickname was "Rabbit" because every time he sees a policeman he runs like a rabbit and hides. He said that his daughter had six kids before her 20th birthday because, "She was young and dumb and her husband was just a bum." (An undiscovered poet?) He said that he quit being a vegetarian when he started leaning toward the sun, and that it is hard to be nostalgic because he can't remember anything. He has never suffered from stress, but he feels like he might be a carrier. He looked like he was in terrible physical condition—but he wore a tee-shirt advertising a fancy fitness center.

This morning I was miraculously the recipient of some strange power that gave me the ability to accurately predict what will happen in the future. Before I even opened the closet door to get a shirt to wear, I saw clearly in my mind the exact shirt that I would pick! Sure enough, I picked that shirt! I told my coffee buddies what happened and that I was a Psychic. They didn't see anything to be excited about. They wrote the experience off to some obscure, complicated concept called "Planning." I think they might be jealous.

I felt sorry for an old man who sat leaning on a stop sign on a busy corner of town holding a crudely made sign that read, "Traveling across country, need money for food. Please help." I gave him some money, only to discover that he was on that same corner every day for the next year. He wasn't traveling very fast.

I noticed a sign on an old rundown building that read, "Historic Office for rent." Great marketing idea! "Historic" sounds much better than "old." Maybe old people should be called "Historic People."

Resting— The last time we went shopping at the mall, I was very proud to have found a great parking place. I bragged to my wife, "I'm as close to handicapped as you can get." She replied, "You've got that right." I always try to find a comfortable chair to sit in while my wife shops in the women's clothing department. In the past, I sat on one of the stools at the perfume counter. I quit that because I just couldn't overcome the temptation to try out all of the different sprays. Now I sit in a chair located just outside of the dressing rooms. Old ladies walk by and give me sweet, patronizing smiles. Old men give me friendly greetings and express sympathy. On one occasion I made the mistake of commenting, "I think it is too tight," to a complete stranger who was looking in the mirror at herself in a new dress. She responded angrily, "Shut your mouth mister! I don't need your unsolicited opinion." She was right, I have no credentials to be a judge of women in dresses, but I thought she wanted my opinion when she glanced at me when she first came out. I better just concentrate on trimming my fingernails and keep quiet. I should have learned that lesson when we killed a cricket in our house. If he would have had enough sense to be quiet, we would have never found him.

One of my buddies had difficulty walking very far without stopping to catch up on his oxygen. He and I were walking through a department store toward the coffee shop when we stopped so he could catch up on oxygen. We happened to be in the middle of the ladies underwear department! A polite sales clerk walked up to us and said, "Can I help you gentlemen find something?" My buddy replied, "No thanks, we just came here to sit and visit. You should put some chairs or a bench in here."

I like to "People Watch" while I pass the time drinking coffee and visiting with my bench buddies. We made up a game called "Miss America." Everyone knows that you can't judge a book by its cover and that prejudice is wrong. But we also know the importance of first impressions. When we play "Miss America" our impression of persons is not based on any particular predetermined objective set of criteria. We simply gather together all of our prejudices, biases, preferences, and likes and dislikes and make a quick, on-the-spot subjective evaluation. Some men prefer women who are heavy, have long hair, are tall, and mature. Other guys like thin ladies with short hair. Being retired from the education profession, I am accustomed to assigning grades to kids. When we play "Miss America," we arbitrarily rate adult women in our minds as they pass our bench using the following scale: (1) sickening (2) very ugly (3) ugly (4) below average (5) average (6) above average (7) pretty (8) beautiful (9) very beautiful (10) Miss America. We make allowances for age, and give extra points if the lady is smiling. I gave my wife a 10 when she came by to say she was ready to head for home. I know I'm prejudiced when it comes to her. I hope there isn't some old lady sitting on a bench rating men as I walk by. I'd hate to think how she would rate me! I'll pull in my stomach and keep smiling. That might help.

It would be fun and enlightening to get a bunch of my bench buddies together out at the mall to compare our rating systems. We could all sit on benches, with yellow scratch pads, and rate each woman as she emerges from the escalator. The activity could even lead to some higher math as we would need to arrive at a mean, mode, and median. A women's auxiliary probably would soon be organized to rate men. National and international organizations would follow. When the activity reached the inevitable competitive stage, people who judged livestock in 4-H when they were kids would probably dominate the purple ribbons.

I Made Him What He Is—I was relaxing on a bench when an old out-of-work drunk bum recognized me as his former principal. He looked and smelled terrible! He "complimented" me by saying, "You were my favorite teacher. Everything I am today, I owe to you. There is no telling where I would be today without your influence!" And I had thought that I had as much influence on kids as a plate of muffins! He complained about how dark it was. He just needed to take off his dark glasses. I really hate to accept all of the credit! He shared his dream of getting rich by becoming the CEO of a "Bathroom on Wheels" business. He explained that homeless and disabled persons can't afford to build "Handicapped Accessible" restrooms, so when they needed to go they would telephone his company and a toilet would be on its way. I asked him how this would work when they didn't have a home to come to, a telephone to call on, and money to pay with, and what would happen if they needed it immediately. He smirked and told me that I needed to "Start thinking outside of the box." He said that the bar advertised "Free Beer Tomorrow" but the sign had been up for two weeks and tomorrow, like the horizon, always recedes as one draws nearer. I got cold while sitting on a bench in the park and I commented to a nearby teenager, "It is sure cool here." He replied, "If you think this place is cool man, you should see the park on the other side of town."

Signs— I saw a sign that said, "Now Hiring, all positions." I guess they want workers who can work standing, sitting, and lying down. Another sign said, "Must be 21 to enter." Does that mean that people of all other ages can't come in? A sign outside of a carwash said, "Walk-ins welcome." I wondered how that would be possible. It seems to me that it wouldn't make much sense to walk-in to a car wash. Wouldn't you have to drive your car in to get it washed? And what about the handicapped who can't walk in? Another sign said, "You Are Here." How did the sign maker know where I was before I even went there? And finally, I saw what I thought was a tombstone in the front yard of a house that said, "Art Frames." I thought that some poor guy named Arthur Frames had died and was buried there. It turns out that it was a sign advertising frames for art work.

T-shirts have become walking billboards. Today I was sitting on a bench at the mall and saw a teenager wearing a shirt with the 1992 Kansas City Chiefs schedule printed on its back. Another kid wore a shirt with, "Dole—Kemp in '96" printed on it. Some kids even wear pep club shirts from other schools that they got at garage sales. It is almost impossible to buy just a plain shirt, with a pocket, without something written on it. An extremely fat and ugly woman waddled down the sidewalk wearing a T-shirt with the following written on it: "XXL Athletic Department, Go Dogs." Why would she want to advertise that she is large sized and looks like a dog? Another T-shirt read, "I was picked last in P.E. class."

Back in the 80s I purchased a T-shirt at a reunion of my mother's side of the family that had "*Johnson Reunion*" printed on it. When I was involved in athletics in college I wore jerseys with, *Bethany Swedes*, printed on them. I saw a shirt in a store that had, "OLD NAVY" written on it. I was discharged from the Navy back in 1956, so I thought the shirt was specially made for me. I bought it and expected to get lots of respect as a veteran when I wore it. Much to my chagrin I soon discovered that this was a new brand of clothing and every kid in the mall had one on. You sure see lots of Ralph Lauren and Tommy Hilfiger family descendants wearing family reunion shirts. Everybody seems to have a tattoo now. "Tattoo Hump Day" is not far off—the day in history when as many people have a tattoo as those who don't.

Breakfast Feast— Two of my close friends, a married couple, enjoy eating breakfast at a wide variety of restaurants. A new motel opened up out on the edge of town, and my friends thought that they would give it a try. They walked in the front door, found the serving line, and helped themselves to a great meal. They enjoyed themselves so much that they decided they would recommend the place to all of their friends. After finishing a leisurely meal they asked the waiter, who had taken good care of them, where the cashier was located. He very pleasantly said, "Oh, there is no extra charge for breakfast, it comes with your room." They were shocked and tried to pay, but couldn't get anyone to understand. They quietly left the premises.

The Hippopotamus—One of my Bench Buddies worried that he might be losing his memory. He was hospitalized for a short time so he could be given a series of tests. His grandchildren visited him and gave him a stuffed hippopotamus as a gift. The tests began with some very simple questions—like what city he lived in. Later the questions got more complex. He was asked what he had eaten for supper the night before, when he had last showered, etc. His wife was in the room observing the questioning and she was proud of how well he was doing. Then he was asked what he was doing immediately prior to taking the test. He calmly replied, "I was in my room playing with my hippopotamus." The psychologist looked startled until his wife explained the answer.

A Bad Day—My Buddy Bernie called and told me that he had experienced a bad day. First, he could hardly see out of his right eye. He called the eye doctor and made an appointment for 2:00 PM. Then he decided to mulch the leaves in his yard with his riding mower, but it wouldn't start. He tried everything but to no avail. He got some old boards to serve as ramps, pushed the mower into the bed of his truck, and took it to a shop. The mechanic put some gas in it and it started fine!

When his wife came home for lunch he told her about his eye problem. She said, "I wonder if it has anything to do with the glasses lens on the table by the bed." Sure enough, the right lens of his glasses had fallen out and his right eye had been looking through no lens. All is well that ends well. It reminded me of the time when Bernie lost his glasses while fishing in the creek. He found them six months later….a half mile downstream. Bernie saves money by turning off the ignition of his car at the top of hills and coasting until his car comes to a complete stop. Some fellow motorists get angry and don't seem to understand his logic!

Elda— Female residents at the local home for the elderly were upset because an old man had been going up and down the halls in the middle of the night knocking on doors. They installed a surveillance camera to catch him in the act so they could evict him. Elda, a beautiful ninety year old lady, with a sharp sense of humor and a twinkle in her eye, said, "I put a note on my door that said, 'knock louder and wait a while, I can't hear very well and I'm slow.'" She can flawlessly play any tune that you request on the organ and piano. She plays the organ for a worship service at the home on Sunday mornings. Visiting ministers come in to direct the service. The management thought they were doing her a great favor by getting a new organ. She good-naturedly accepted it but quietly commented that she felt more comfortable with the old organ and wished they could find some excuse to get it back. Her concern was heightened one Sunday when she accidentally hit the rumba rhythm button on the new organ and played "Amazing Grace" to the rumba beat. The visiting minister didn't appear to have a sense of humor. She also told me about the time when she took in two stray cats, a male and a female, because she felt sorry for them. She didn't want any more cats so she took the female to the veterinarian to have it spayed. After cutting into the cat, the vet discovered that she had already been spayed. Elda wondered what that cat would have said if it could have talked.

She said that she was once chosen to represent her neighbors to protest against the "red water" in the municipal water supply. She made an emotional presentation to the city council and the mayor. She held up her stained underwear to demonstrate what happened to white clothing when washed in the rusty water, and passed the underwear around so each council member could see up close what she was talking about. Her presentation was aired on three local television stations and she was the talk-of-the-town. That was the high-point of her "brief" career as a community activist.

Elda's husband died years ago, but she still enjoys telling stories about him. He had received notice that, unless he volunteered to join the military service within a week, he would be drafted into the army. He didn't want that to happen, so he went to the recruiting station to join the Navy. The Navy recruiting officer was out to lunch, so the Air Force recruiter took the opportunity to convince him to join the Air Force. That changed his life completely and resulted in his meeting Elda. This experience taught her that when someone thinks they are criticizing a person by saying that they are "Out to lunch" they should take the comment as a compliment. Elda got some vitamins that were specially made to meet the needs of women. When her husband insisted on taking them she told him that his voice would probably get higher pitched. When she complained about the house they lived in, he took her for a ride in the car and pointed out how bad some of the houses under the bridge were.

She bought some ice cream at the supermarket and read on the package, "Home-made in Oakland, California, since 1928." She laughed when she said that she had a vision of little old men and ladies sitting on a stool out in the farmyard in the center of Oakland, California, turning a crank on an ice cream maker. What a lady!

She said that one of her friends had repeatedly experienced the problem of falling out of bed at night. She thought the solution to this would be to cut the legs off of her bed so she wouldn't get hurt falling so far. She did that, and then discovered that it was almost impossible for her to get in and out of her bed. A new bed with rails was the answer.

Elda always kept the door open when she used the bathroom. She claimed that she had inherited this practice from her mother and grandmother. Her grandma used an outdoor outhouse. Wasps often built nests under the outhouse toilet bench. Things were going fine until one day a wasp flew off the nest and stung grandma on her rear. Grandma also claimed to see snakes under the outhouse seat. She kept the door open so she could escape fast if she needed to. This practice of keeping the door open was passed on to Elda's mom and then to her. Now her grown children, and even her grandchildren, do the same. They don't understand exactly why they leave the door open, but it is a family trait.

She complained that a lady down the hall from her died in the middle of the night and made such a terrible racket that it kept her awake half of the night. How inconsiderate some people are! The least she could have done is die quietly!

Elda's children thought it would be nice to hire a lady to clean her apartment once every two weeks. Elda didn't want to have the cleaning lady think that she was messy, so she always did a good job of cleaning before the lady arrived. The lady complained that she had nothing to clean!

Bad Timing— One of my Bench Buddies told me that his son returned from his vacation and discovered that some company got mixed up and replaced his garage doors instead of his next door neighbor's. It worked out great because the garage door company was so embarrassed that they let him keep them without paying for them. He wishes now that they had put new siding on his house. His wife wasn't so lucky. She was scheduled to have the doctor examine her large intestines and colon. The doctor instructed her to not eat anything for twenty-four hours before the exam and to clean out her bowels by swallowing some terrible tasting medicine. She did all of this, and then discovered that her exam wasn't until the next week. It reminded me of the time when my buddy agreed to mow a lady's lawn and mowed her next door neighbor's lawn by mistake. He never did get paid for that job.

Unsolicited Help— One of my buddies went out in his front yard to pull some weeds on a hot summer evening. His neighbor saw him lying on the lawn, moving only occasionally, and thought he must have fallen and couldn't get up. He came over to see if he needed help. Another bench buddy waited in his car while his wife went into a sewing supply store. He was tired, so he put his head down on the steering wheel to rest. Soon a large crowd gathered around his car and an ambulance was called. Although he is retired, this same guy wanted a little extra money so he applied for a job as a part time custodian at a hospital. He thought for sure that he had the job because only three people applied—him, a one-legged guy, and a hippie. He didn't get the job.

I Overheard the Following Comments While Sitting on a Bench at the Mall—"I bought my wife a cemetery lot for Christmas and she got mad. I'm the one who should be mad, because she never used it; just like the dishwasher that I bought her, it has never been used either"— "I better go check to see if my car is locked. I've got some Bibles in the back seat that I would hate to have stolen."—Grandma to a young girl, "Do you want some mustard?" The young girl replies, "No." Grandma responds, "What do you mean No! Now take some mustard!"—"Every year on December 24th I go to the *Everything for a Dollar* store to buy my wife a present. It is always crowded with last minute shoppers. Why do so many stupid people wait until the last minute to do their shopping?"—"When I was younger I thought that it would be dumb to have plastic surgery done. Yesterday I looked at my reflection in the mirror and was shocked at how many wrinkles I have. I changed my mind about plastic surgery."— "My Aunt and Uncle are not very smart and even worse spellers. They had three kids. The birth certificates read, *Kinnith, Pasty, and Heaven Lee"*— "The preacher picked me to read the scripture at church. I didn't like what it said so I changed it."

My Coffee Buddy told me that he suffered a serious cut years ago when working in the field cutting hay. He went to the doctor to have it stitched up, but he cut the stitches out himself two weeks later rather than pay the doctor to do it. He went to have his driver's license renewed and they took a picture of him for identification. When he got home he compared it to his four year old expired license. He had the same shirt on in both pictures; only it was a little lighter color now. His neighbor went on vacation and left his dog at home. In the middle of the night it started to rain and lightning and thunder. The excited, scared, and dripping wet dog jumped through the screen of his bedroom window and got in bed with him. My buddy said that when he was in the army he spent so much time napping in his bed that his buddies nicknamed him "Horizontal Smith."

Years ago my buddy worked at a weight station for the Highway Patrol. A very large truck came in that had too much weight on the front axle but room to spare on the rear axle. He told the driver that he would have to move some of the contents to the rear of the truck. The driver slowly backed up, started backing faster and faster, and suddenly slammed on the brakes! There was a loud noise as the contents of the truck shifted to the rear. What a mess the inside of that truck must have been! But the truck now passed the weight test on both axles.

He asked me if I remembered his son, Bobby. I had Bobby in school quite a few years ago, and remembered him as a borderline problem kid who messed around with drugs. He was the brightest member of his family… but that is like being the smartest bear in the zoo. I said, "Yes, I remember him, how is he doing now?" He said, "Bobby got busted two nights ago." I assumed that he meant that Bobby had gotten arrested for using drugs. I said "Oh, how did that happen?" He explained, "Some guy came up to him in a bar out west of town and just hit him in the jaw and busted it!"

He described in agonizing detail how some young punk had communicated to him that it was not appropriate to blow his nose while driving slowly in the fast lane on the interstate highway. He was fumbling in his back pocket to get his handkerchief out when the guy behind him started honking, waving one of his fingers around in the air, and roaring his motor. His wife helped by interpreting the sign language.

I can identify with him because I'm one of those old-timers who don't feel completely dressed if I don't have a handkerchief in my back pocket. Every morning I go through the same routine. I use a clean handkerchief to wipe off the lens of my glasses, clean out my ears, and then blow my nose. I found out the hard way that these procedures must be done in that exact order.

Doctor's Office— I was sitting in the doctors' waiting room reading the exciting article, "*Dealing with Acid Reflux,*" in the magazine, "*Digestive Health and Nutrition.*" An old man made his wife wait so he could watch the end of "The Price is Right" on the waiting room TV, even though they had both completed their doctor visits. A sign on the wall advised anyone who felt that they had been discriminated against because of a disability to call an 800 number in Washington D.C. It reminded me of the sign on the wall of a multi-purpose room of a school that served as both a lunchroom and gymnasium. It gave an 800 number to call to complain about the federally funded lunch program. A dad, who felt the basketball referee had done a poor job, called the Secretary of Agriculture in Washington to complain.

Dolly Parton— The entire atmosphere of the hospital laboratory waiting room changed from silence and gloom to cheerfulness and excitement when a nurse called out the name, "Molly Barton." The old men who were waiting in wheel chairs suffered from hearing loss and thought the nurse had yelled, "Dolly Parton." They all perked up and looked around the room in great anticipation. Then a nurse ruined all of the fun by clarifying the matter. The incident helped to brighten up the day for a little while. It also provided everyone with something humorous to tell their buddies when they returned to the rest home. The bright sunshine of optimism had shone brightly; if only for an instant. Then a nurse called out one old man's name and he asked his wife, "Is that me?

Coffee and Tea— I was just trying to be helpful. The waitress was busy, and we needed refills, so I got the pot and filled all of the mugs. Soon it was discovered that I had poured hot tea into the coffee cups. Coffee mixed with tea doesn't taste very good. The waitress had rings on all of her fingers. She explained that she wears them because if she leaves them at home they might get stolen. Speaking of rings, a man at a pot luck supper said that his grandma lost her wedding ring while planting her garden. She and others searched for the ring, sifting through the dirt, but couldn't find it. Several years later, while harvesting her garden produce, she pulled a carrot up from the ground. To her surprise she found that the carrot had grown through her ring. One of my buddies told about losing his billfold when plowing a field when he was a kid. He looked all over for it, but didn't find it until he plowed it up the next year.

Losing Weight— When a very fat lady walked up to the bench I was sitting on, I made what I considered to be a welcoming comment that I had made to other people many times. I said, "Sit down and take a load off of your feet." I meant no harm, but she seemed offended. After she sat down next to me, and the bench sank much lower but didn't break, I tried to be nice and said, "Do you have enough room?" Again, that must have been the wrong thing to say. She soon calmed down and admitted that she desperately needed to lose weight. She had resigned herself to being heavy because she believed in evolution, and that she was therefore related to bears. Because of this she rationalized that she was genetically programmed to gain weight at the beginning of winter each year. She believed that when people lose weight it goes up into the atmosphere. Being an avid environmentalist, she was concerned about the air pollution that her losing weight would cause.

Friendly Conversation—I was trying to be friendly and struck up a conversation with an elderly lady. I asked her where she grew up. I can usually count on that question to lead to a long monologue about how things were years ago. She replied, "I grew up right smack dab in the center of Kansas; halfway between Omaha and Des Moines." That was the end of that! Another lady volunteered that her husband drove a huge semi-trailer from coast to coast, and that she went with him quite often. She said that when her husband got tired, he turned over the steering wheel to her and crawled back in the sleeping quarters to take a nap. She said that she could steer the rig, but didn't know how to use the brakes or shift. The thought of that big truck, with her at the controls, cruising down the highway at 70 miles per hour, scared me. She said that her husband purchased his false teeth in England. Both the upper and lower set had magnets imbedded backward in them so they would repel each other and keep them in place. That worked well, but he could only close his mouth with tremendous effort.

The Execution Party—I shared a bench at the mall with an older man and we started to discuss our military service. We talked about how many close friends we had made while in the military service. He said that he had recently received a phone call from one of his old Army buddies and had been invited to Dallas, Texas, for his execution. I didn't ask if reservations were required or if refreshments would be served. He said that he had recently been sick and got a hospital bill for $450,000. The hospital set up a "payment plan" that would have him 138 years old when the debt would be paid off. He recently received a traffic ticket for driving too slow. He was driving his riding lawnmower across a long bridge, pulling his wife behind in a grocery cart. The traffic backed up for miles. He said that last year the 4th of July was on Thursday so "I just made a long weekend of it." On "President's Day," the court house, post office, schools, and library were closed. He thought it would be a good day for him to "take off" also, but he didn't have anything to "take off from." He complained that, "Everybody else gets to experience a three day weekend. Why can't I? I think I'll write a letter to my congressman to complain about this problem. It is surely George Bush's fault!" He was upset because it didn't rain as much at his home as the weather man on TV said it did. The next time we visited he said that he was embarrassed to admit that it could be because he installed his rain gauge under a tree.

Dark Veins—In our youth we were cautioned that "beauty is only skin deep." Now I hope the same is true for bruises, wrinkles, and moles. My driver's license picture looks like a "before" picture in a plastic surgery ad.

From a distance, we couldn't tell if an older lady had a tattoo on her leg or dark colored veins that looked like a bird of some kind. I went closer to talk to her and found out that she had varicose veins. She told me that since she retired she has had trouble knowing what day of the week it is. Every day seems like Saturday except "Trash Day" and Sunday. Sometimes she even gets those mixed up. Once she was confused and dressed up to go to church on a Saturday. She didn't want to waste being all dressed up, so she looked in the newspaper and found a funeral she could attend. She attends lots of funerals so that when she dies those who died will return the favor and attend her funeral. That way she won't have to worry that nobody will attend her funeral. She also told me that she gets the daily newspaper free. She worked out a deal with her next door neighbor to pass the paper on to her the following day. Not only that; she gets to keep 100% of the money she gets when she recycles the newspaper! She is in no hurry to get the news, because, "I've had enough excitement in my life already." This rationale gave me the idea that it would be nice if we could rotate the dates of Christmas and New Years. Gifts are cheaper after December 25th and if Christmas was on January 1st lots of money could be saved. Also, I often wonder why we wish each other "Merry" Christmas and "Happy" New Year. Why not "Happy" Christmas and "Merry" New Year? And what kind of a Fourth of July do we want our friends to have?

Pest Control—One of my coffee buddies grew up during the 1940s in a small town in North-Central Kansas. One year his high school Future Farmers of America chapter (FFA) had a project with the purpose of ridding the area of farm pests. Members were encouraged to trap and kill rodents and bring the carcasses to school. They would earn different amounts of points, depending upon whether it was a mouse or a rat, and how long the body measured. The project had to be discontinued because of two problems. First, serious disagreement evolved concerning methods of measuring; should a thin long tailed critter count more than a heavier one with a short tail? Second, teachers, bus drivers, and the principal didn't think it was in good taste to bring such a smelly and disgusting thing to school. Another great idea goes down the drain, but don't worry, like all concepts in educational circles, it will be recycled and rise again.

Talking about pest control, I have developed a very friendly relationship with my pest control technician. He comes to service our home at least once a year, and always hangs around after he finishes inspecting the house to visit. I told him that our school district had a new program in place to deal with bullying. He is a very intelligent and wise guy, so I was pleased when he told me that he knew the best way for kids to deal with bullies. I listened intently because I assumed that he was aware of new methods of conflict resolution or peer mediation. He said, "The kid being picked on should walk up to the bully, look him straight in the eye and hit him with his fist as hard as he can smack dab on the nose." I decided not to pass this suggestion on to the school district. He invited me to his daughter's wedding and the reception following the ceremony. The reception is going to be pot-luck. I wish I had thought of that when my daughters got married.

The Car Horn—One of my buddies had trouble sleeping early one morning so he got out of bed and dressed for the day. He put his billfold and keys in his pants pocket so he would be ready to go out to eat breakfast when his wife got ready. He sat down to read the morning newspaper and noticed that a car horn somewhere in his neighborhood was honking. He thought, "That noise is disturbing my concentration. I wish that the idiot that owns the car would stop his car from honking." Soon his wife came downstairs and asked him to go outside and find out where the honking was coming from. She was preparing to call the police and register a complaint. He went outside and, much to his dismay, the honking was coming from inside of his own garage. He had inadvertently hit the "horn" button on his automatic car key in his pocket. He went inside and told his wife that he had discovered where the honking was coming from and the owner had taken care of it. It reminded him of how nervous he had been when he had to renew his driver's license the last time. He didn't want them to think that his advancing age affected his mental sharpness. He parked outside of the testing place and accidentally hit that same horn button.

Headache—One of my bench buddies consulted the doctor about his headache. The doctor told him to take the pain reliever "Aleve." He didn't hear well and told his wife that the doctor told him he had to take a leave, so they went on a vacation. When I told him that I missed him when he didn't attend our coffee group last week he said, "I was not gone, I was just not here." That explained his absence I guess.

I'm Not Leo—I sat down on a bench in the mall to rest while my wife Myra shopped. Three older ladies walked by and one of them looked at me and said, "Hi, Leo." They walked on past and I didn't have time to explain that I was not Leo. They came around again and the same lady said, "Where is Edith today?" She didn't wait for my answer. On the next round she said, "Aren't you going to walk today, Leo?" I thought that I had better leave and not further the misunderstanding. I went into a store and found Myra. We walked out of the store together and met the group of ladies. They gave us a very surprised and disgusted look. Leo was out with a strange lady! They could hardly wait to tell Edith.

Dogs, Snoring, and Moles—A Bench Buddy's wife demanded that he buy a watch dog as a security measure. The dog got along fine the first day and it looked like it would fit nicely into the family. When he and his wife came home on the second day, the dog attacked them and wouldn't let them in their own house. The dog had a short memory. He called the dog-catcher to take in his own dog. His wife was so angry at him that she vowed to only talk to herself and the family cat, because, "The cat is the only one in this family who really listens to me."

He shared with our group that he and his wife had been very embarrassed the last time they stayed in a motel. He snored so loud that it woke up all of the other guests in the motel in the middle of the night. They reported to the desk clerk that a loud noise was coming from the vicinity of his room. They guessed that a furnace motor had gone bad. He heard a loud knock on his door, opened it, and in some magic way the loud roar stopped. His wife knew all the time what had happened, but she had adjusted to his snoring years ago.

He said that a friend from a nearby rural town told him that the best way to rid your yard of moles is to have a two-keg beer party, and ask all of the guests to relieve themselves all over the yard in the dark. I wonder what the invitations to the party looked like! It would probably drive the local dogs crazy when they sniffed around the next morning. But, if the procedure kills moles, I guess it will soon be standard practice everywhere.

An old lady told me that she had heard that moles don't like movable yard art and will move on if they see it. Every time she saw evidence of a mole she installed new, and increasingly obnoxious, pieces of movable yard art randomly around her yard. The yard was a tourist attraction, but was a real challenge to mow. She just let the weeds grow. She is planning to get a copyright on the following toilet paper idea: "Stick the plunger on the wall so the handle extends out about 6 inches in front of your nose. Store toilet paper rolls on the handle and place elbows on the rolls and take a nap."

Birds and Squirrels—One of my buddies spends lots of time sitting in a lawn chair in his back yard where he observes birds use the bird feeder that he made from scrap wood and junk corrugated metal. What an exciting life! One day he counted seven different squirrels. They had become a nuisance by jumping onto the metal roof of the bird feeder and crawling down to eat the bird food. They made a mess! After much deliberation and contemplation, he decided that he must do something to end this. He remembered how much enjoyment he experienced watching his bug zapper in action last summer before his neighbor ruined the fun by encroaching on his territory by putting up another zapper next door to him. The next several days were devoted to building an elaborate electrical system and hooking it up to the metal roof of the bird feeder. He watched with much anticipation as the first squirrel jumped onto the roof. He switched 120 volts of electricity on. The squirrel immediately felt a severe shock and fell to the ground. After a few minutes it rolled over onto his feet and limped off. Squirrels don't communicate very well with each other, so each of the seven squirrels went through the same learning experience. He couldn't devote all of his time to this endeavor, so he just left the current on all day. The system worked great, but he neglected to consider that what works for squirrels also works for birds.

Another bench buddy said that he had attempted to solve the squirrel problem by putting his bird feeder on top of a metal pole. Much to his surprise, some of the more athletically inclined squirrels found a way to climb up the pole. He solved that by coating the pole with Crisco oil. This is a wonderful example of another "Bench buddy problem solving technique."

Trip to Detroit—A bench buddy said that back in the 60s he decided that he needed to leave town because he owed lots of people money, his former wife continually bothered him about helping raise their kids, and he didn't have a job. He had a 1952 Ford that was in very poor mechanical condition. He enlisted the help of a fellow shade tree mechanic and the two of them prepared the car for the 600 mile trip to Detroit. His buddy told him that the car would last three days at the most. He drove 80 mph all the way to Detroit so he could get there within the allotted three days. He sent his family a postcard—a picture of a 1952 Ford.

The COBRA Trip—Several times a year, I accompany a dozen of my retired teacher buddies on trips around Kansas. The tongue-in-cheek name of our group is "COBRA." (Corps of Brave and Righteous Americans) Recently we stopped for breakfast at "Luther's Smokehouse" in LeRoy, Kansas. A sign on the wall read, "Martin Luther—Owner, Shirley Luther—Boss." This place is a great example of humor in its purest form; humor that is not caustic, racist, offensive, or embarrassing. Neither is it comedy or showmanship. Instead, it is the ability to look at the simple things of life and find in them a reason to smile and a cause to chuckle—and more importantly, the ability to laugh at oneself. Installed in the restroom, next to the toilet, was an old antique parking meter. A lamp consisting of a lady's legs for a stand and a short skirt for the shade graced the room. On the wall was mounted humorous things like: a small piece of wood carved to look like a roof with thumb tacks under it (a tax shelter), a quarter glued to a piece of wood next to a wooden hammer (a quarter-pounder), and a round piece of wood about the size of a fifty cent piece with "2 it" written on it. (So you can do those things that you said you will do if you ever get *around to it*.)

We struck up a conversation with a delightful group of older men. They were proud to let us know that Babe Ruth's New York Yankee roommate grew up in LeRoy, Kansas, and that they would be happy to take us to meet one of his second nieces. We declined the invitation. One of the men was a retired minister. He told us, "I was a dry land minister, a Methodist. The Baptists use lots of water to baptize, Lutherans use a cup full, but we only use a damp rag." He reported that a few days ago he almost fell and hurt himself. When he arrived to visit with his buddies he hung his cane on a peg on the wall. When he got up to leave, he leaned on his cane and lunged forward, almost falling to the floor. One of his buddies had shortened his cane!

Air Bag—My buddy bought a new car, but he doesn't like it. He said that every time he starts it up it flashes, **"Air Bag!"** on the dash board. He admits that he talks too much, but he doesn't appreciate his own car calling him names.

Questioning Dad—One of my buddies told me that when he was a kid his dad required him to "rotate his belt" every day so it would hang straight down when hung on a hook. For many years he put his belt on clockwise on odd numbered days and counter-clockwise on even numbered days. Last year he got so sick that he couldn't make the change every day, and to his surprise nothing drastic happened. He is now in the process of questioning everything his dad told him.

Trip to Sweden—We traveled to Sweden in the summer of 2000. One of our elderly fellow travelers, Ole Swenson, was a fascinating guy who became one of my favorite bench buddies. Ole woke up early one morning and decided to use the bicycle parked outside of the hotel to ride around and explore the area. He returned to the hotel and told the desk clerk, "I rode the hotel's bike this morning, how much do I owe you?" The hotel clerk replied, with a smile on her face, "We don't have any bicycles!" Ole was embarrassed and thankful that he hadn't been picked up by the police and charged with stealing a bike. Wherever we went in Sweden, he looked in trash bins for discarded barbed wire, old nails, and antique hardware. He collected these as a hobby. While the rest of us were touring cultural centers, Ole was visiting hardware stores. He picked up a catalog in one hardware store and, later on the bus, he showed it to our Swedish guide. She laughed and told Ole that it clearly states in Swedish on the cover of the catalog, "This catalog is not to leave the store." We listened carefully for a police siren, but Ole had made a clean getaway. He said that he was 21 years old before he learned that nails were not bent when you buy them brand new. He had only experienced nails that had been previously used and never had seen brand new ones.

Chapter Three
Down-to-Earth
Educational Philosophy

The Battered Bike Collage— A man who lives several miles outside of our city limits hates bicyclists. When he drives home, and bike riders get in front of him, he must slow down to almost a stop. He lives on a hilly and winding road with no shoulders, so it is difficult to pass these pests. Persons who come out from the city to have fun riding a bike in the country really upset him. He doesn't have that same hatred for slow moving farm vehicles because he understands that they are necessary. He constructed a metal collage, like a huge totem pole, near his mailbox out by the road to demonstrate how he feels about bicycles and those who ride them. It is made up of a mass of battered bike parts welded together over a toilet stool. I heard about a battered bedpan collage built by a guy who was mad at hospitals. Likewise, many people harbor strong negative feelings about some other group of people because of bad experiences in the past; it could be doctors, teachers, dentists, lawyers, preachers, or politicians. They build psychological "battered something collages" in their minds to express negative feelings instead of physical monuments in their yards. We should understand and be philosophical about this and not get caught up in doing it.

The Persistent Paraplegic Ant— I was soaking in the bath tub and noticed an ant crawling up the wall. I reached up, squashed it with a washrag, and placed it on the edge of the tub to discard when I got out. It slowly moved along the edge of the tub and fell on the floor. I hit it again, picked it up with a piece of toilet paper, and threw it into the toilet. While brushing my teeth I watched this amazing ant, by now definitely a paraplegic with only his top part working, crawl off the toilet paper island, swim over to the edge of the toilet, and begin crawling up the steep slope. I had come to admire this persistent creature so much that I decided to rescue it and turn it loose outside. Before I could do this my grandson flushed the toilet. I saw the ant desperately grab hold of a piece of toilet paper and ride it down the swirling torrent. I was saddened by this turn of events but considered the matter closed. Several days later, while sitting on my backyard patio, I could hardly believe my eyes. I saw an ant crawl along the patio. I recognized it as my persistent paraplegic friend, smiled, and wished him (or maybe her) well.

One of my bench buddies told me that tomato plants sometimes grow next to the sewer lateral lines in his backyard. He claims that tomato seeds that had been passed through his digestive system or garbage disposal, drain pipes, and septic tank, and into the lateral lines in his backyard survived and formed productive plants.

These two examples of persistent, tough ants and tomatoes remind me of some of the kids that I worked with over the years in school. For some unknown reason, some kids are survivors. They are able to overcome huge obstacles and extremely difficult situations in their environment, and not only survive but grow stronger as a result. I have witnessed kids grow up to be productive adults who lived in poverty and whose parents were drug addicts and drunks and gave them almost no nurturing. These are the real heroes of America!

One high school boy's only means of transportation to and from football practice and games was by foot. Sometimes he had to run the three miles to keep from being punished for being late. He developed into the best conditioned athlete on the team, was honored as an all-state selection, got a college scholarship, and became a very successful teacher.

The Carousel, or merry-go-round as we call it in Kansas, is the essence of joy, delight, and pleasure. Each of us, no matter how old we may be, has a child within us yearning to ride it. The music, the motion, and an almost magical feeling of being somehow in touch with all of those who have ridden in the past; all of these contribute to an atmosphere of absolute ecstasy. It is fun to watch a child riding on it, but it is even more fun to watch parents watching their children riding on it. I watched a group of mentally handicapped adults and adolescents riding it, going up and down, round and round, giggling, petting their horse, laughing out loud, and with smiles as wide as their face. Maybe they were not handicapped after all! Could it be that those who are too cool or dignified to ride a carousel are the ones who are handicapped?

The Gumball Machine Complex—My wife and I were driving our granddaughter, Heather, age four to Sunday School. Heather and three other grandchildren were settled in the car when I asked Heather, "How are you today, Heather?" Heather replied angrily, "Not Beary Good! Erin got three things out of the gumball machine and I only got two." According to Heather's mother, their family had visited friends in Wichita a week earlier and the gumball incident had occurred. Heather had not mentioned it since but had been visibly upset at times. The incident was a minor one in the eyes of everyone but Heather. She had been quietly mad for a week.

In every classroom there are students who are experiencing the Gumball Machine Complex. They feel that they have been gypped in some way. They only got a little bit of something and they see others who got more. Maybe other girls are cheerleaders and they are not. Possibly they feel that they got the short end of the stick because their families are not economically well off. They may feel that they are physically weaker or less attractive than others. Sometimes the problem could be something that to others seems very minor but is very important to the person who feels gypped. The condition can be a very mild case causing only a bad attitude for a short period of time or so serious that long-term difficulties develop. We should always be alert to the possibility that others with whom we have contact may be experiencing the Gumball Machine Complex and help them deal with it.

Only a Drop in the Bucket. We have all heard educators express the feeling that the influence they have on students doesn't matter much because it is *"only a drop in the bucket."* They reason that they have students at school for only a very small percentage of their lives. At the secondary level most staff members only have one period of the day to influence any one student. Many teachers are in contact with over a hundred students each day. Administrators feel overwhelmed by the responsibility to influence every student in the school. Educators are by nature sincerely concerned about all of their students, but they wonder how thin they can be spread. They feel frustrated that they can't make more of a difference in each of their student's lives.

The bucket is probably mostly filled by parents—both genetically and by early age contact. What children inherit and learn from their parents may be good, or may be bad, but is definitely dominant over other influences.

The good news is that the bucket is filled one drop at a time. Each and every drop is important. The influence of parents is added to that of one teacher which is added to the influence of other teachers. Then is added the influence of YMCA workers, civic club members, church workers, 4-H club leaders, scout leaders, recreation workers, coaches, and thousands of other persons who have some kind of relationship with the child over a long period of time. Individual drops in the bucket combine to make a large volume. The combined efforts of everyone who lives in any community has a tremendous influence on each individual that lives in that community.

Many of us have been pleasantly surprised when we discover how much influence we have had on individual students. They very rarely tell us because they don't quite know how to. They would be embarrassed and are often not capable of articulating the strong feelings of respect and admiration that they feel. Most adults can look back over their lifetime and pick out individuals who contributed more than just a single drop in their buckets. Most of these individuals that we pick out as influencing us never had any idea that they had made such a great difference. Many of them died not knowing what they had accomplished. We never told them! How sad.

The greatest compliment a person can receive is to be

mentioned as a person who made a difference in the life of an old codger when he engages in rambling reminiscence of his life. Teachers have an opportunity to make a difference that those in other professions do not have. If we act each day in a manner that could result in us being so remembered fifty years from now, we will be successful now.

Just a drop in the bucket. Maybe. But without each drop, the bucket would be less full than it is. We get to our destination one inch at a time. We learn one lesson at a time. Our bucket is filled one drop at a time.

Fork in Your Chair—I've noticed that when you tether a dog, it will spend most of its time at the outer limits of the rope, pulling, barking, and wanting to go further. It is the same with people. No matter how liberal the limits, they are unhappy and spend much of their time and energy complaining and begging to have the limits broadened. Nobody likes people who continually complain, whine, and gripe. It seems like much of what I do in my job involves listening to people tell me what is wrong. Sometimes it seems that the best thing that happens to me is that I get a wrong number phone call. It gets tiresome listening to all of the negative, crybaby stuff. Yesterday I thought I was just being treated to more of the same when my one-year-old granddaughter, Audrey, was expressing her discomfort when we were eating breakfast in a restaurant. We had let her know several times that we didn't like to hear her whine, and were about to take her out to the car for time out, when we noticed that she was sitting on a fork. No one knows how the fork got in her high chair, but removing it was all it took to improve Audrey's disposition. It caused me to wonder how many other people that I had gotten angry at during the last week for complaining had in fact also had a "fork in their chair." The phrase "fork in your chair" has come to mean that you have a *real rather than a perceived grievance.*

Remembering the experience with Audrey helps to keep me from treating all complaints as lacking credibility. Some people and groups of people really do have a "fork in their chair." We need to listen to them and "remove the fork" if we have the power to do so.

Garbage Men and Ditch Diggers— My mom motivated me to do my best back in the 1940s by telling me that if I didn't work hard and succeed in school I would end up being a garbage man or a ditch digger. At that time, persons in those professions were considered to be at the bottom of the occupational ladder. In-sink garbage disposals had not been invented then. People put garbage in cans in the alley to be dumped into stinking trucks. Garbage was real garbage then; not to be confused with its high brow cousin, trash. The possibility of spending a lifetime hanging onto the back of one of those dripping, foul smelling trucks during all kinds of weather and throwing garbage into them if you didn't get your homework done, would motivate even the most passive kid. The ditch digger was the ultimate symbol of physical labor. These two jobs completely lacked dignity and respect. We knew that if we didn't develop our brain, we would end up earning a living by doing back-breaking labor the rest of our life. That possibility no longer exists. Garbage disposals take care of garbage. Trash men drive high priced trucks, use high tech methods of disposal, and are members of the Chamber of Commerce. Ditch diggers are now large equipment operators who demand high salaries. Today, people who don't develop their minds and serve a useful function in society go on welfare. Today's kids don't have the advantage of the possibility of being a garbage man or ditch digger. What a pity!

The Instructional Staff of a School Is like an Orchestra. Each member of both an orchestra and of a school staff is an expert in his particular specialty. Each is well trained, has practiced long and hard, and keeps up with the latest trends in his field of expertise. All individuals play a significant role. Mutual-respect should prevail.

Both an orchestra and a school must have a leader; the director and the principal.

The orchestra leader is usually not better at playing any particular instrument than the individual players that he or she directs. Orchestra members are specialists and experts at playing a particular instrument.

Likewise, the school principal often is not as proficient as the teachers that he directs at performing their specialties. Teachers are likewise experts and specialists at teaching in a particular area of the curriculum and deserve to be respected as such.

Both education and music have three basic elements: *rhythm, harmony, and melody.*

A school staff needs to be on the same schedule, or *rhythm*, of getting things done. Principals must set the beat so that everyone is working together and is "on the same page." Principals must also determine the volume of the entire group and, when the script calls for it, direct specific individuals to do solos and to be featured while the rest of the group plays a background role.

The staffs of both orchestras and schools must work together in *harmony*. Various players are expected to play different notes, but the resulting outcome must be in harmony. All participants must be playing in the same key and major or minor mode. The secret to an orchestra playing in beautiful harmony is that all players do **not** play the exact same note at the exact same time. Some instruments are larger and emit deep, low, mellow tones. Some are smaller and have higher and shriller sounds. Woodwinds, brass, string, and percussion instruments; each has a unique quality to contribute to the overall beautiful sound of an orchestra (its outcome). A school staff needs the same diversity of contribution and a wide range of input from a variety of sources if it is to effectively promote learning (its outcome). If every player in an orchestra plays the same note as the conductor and with the same instrument that the conductor plays, the result will be a monotonous uniformity that lacks beauty and harmony and is not pleasing to the ear. Likewise, if every staff member specializes in the same thing and always takes the same approach to solving problems that the principal takes, the school will lack the vitality needed to adequately meet the needs of a diverse student body.

It is important that members of both orchestras and school staffs be playing the same tune, a *common melody*, and working toward the same objectives as the others in their group.

A building principal must possess the ability to determine when one staff member or department is playing too loud, too soft, or is out of tune. He must have the skill to take whatever action is needed to correct problems. Although he might not be able to do the particular job better than the misfit, he has enough general knowledge to sense discord and when someone is out of tune.

In an orchestra, as in a school, the leader is only as good as the players make him. From the principal's perspective, the great baseball manager's philosophy was right when he said, "Ability is the art of getting credit for all of the home runs somebody else hits." Orchestras are judged by the quality of the sound that they make. The conductor does not personally make any sound whatsoever. Both the conductor and the principal must get the job done through the efforts of others. They both depend on each individual member of their team to perform at the highest possible level of excellence. Individual members of the orchestra, and of the education team, are dependent on the leader to play the role of directing the whole unit so that harmony prevails.

No man is an island unto himself. We depend on each other. We must work as a team.

Middle School—Everyone should take the time, at least once in their lives, to experience firsthand the sounds and sights found exclusively in a Middle School. If you watch carefully you can see the bright light bulb flash in the head of a student as he suddenly grasps an understanding of some concept or idea. You can almost see the eighth grade boys grow, usually one part at a time. If you listen carefully, you can hear the seventh grade girls' busts busting and the ninth grade boys' hormones moaning. Females come into middle school as caterpillars and leave as butterflies. In elementary school, the girls fought to play with the same toy; now in middle school they fight to play with the same boy. You can observe both complete ecstasy and deep depression, on the same day in the same kid. Happy voices, laughs and giggles in the lunchroom, loud screaming in the gymnasium, muffled whispering, and sobs in the girls' restroom (the unofficial or peer counselor's office) combine to create the daily sights and sounds of the middle school. Individual differences are the name of the game. Tapping on the desk, bouncing the leg until the whole room shakes, "We were just playing around," "He did it to me first," "Everyone else does it," playing with food, burping just for fun, boys jumping to touch ceilings, girls looking in the mirror, rummaging around in lockers, tapping on the shoulder and then looking the other way, April Fool's day, not being seen with your mom, pimples, girls at the bus stop waving their arms pretending to be cheerleaders, bumping each other off of the end of the bench, acting cool one minute and as excited as a kindergartner the next. This is middle school!

Sports Tourette's Syndrome—Some spectators at athletic events made school administration difficult. They appeared to be suffering from what I call, "Sports Tourette's Syndrome." These are otherwise kind and gentle persons, who in their daily life wouldn't think of behaving in an obnoxious or offensive manner, who suddenly blurt out loud, despicable, and intolerable sounds directed at game officials or the opposition. One prime example is a small town mortician that I often observed in action at my relatives' funerals acting very reserved and dignified. On Friday nights he turned into a totally different person—one who obviously suffered from "Sports Tourette's Syndrome."

God's Telephone Number— A kindergarten teacher told me that after more than thirty-five years she finds that she is even more emotionally moved by some of the things kids say than she was on the first day she taught. She has stood under the same tree supervising kids on the playground for all of those years. She feels as though that tree is one of her best friends, and that the two of them share some very emotionally overwhelming memories.

One day a sweet little kindergarten boy in her class was having a bad day. No matter how hard he tried, everything seemed to go wrong. With tears in his eyes, in a soft voice he asked his teacher, "Do you know God's telephone number? I need to call my daddy." His father had recently suddenly and unexpectedly died. She asked a kindergarten student, "What is your name?" He responded sadly, "I'm Nobody, you can just call me Nobody."

A second grade boy woke up in the morning and found his mother on the floor unconscious. He tried unsuccessfully to wake her up. He couldn't call 911, like he usually does, because his mother didn't pay the phone bill and it had been taken out. He dressed his little three year old brother and walked with him to the bus stop. When they arrived at school he politely asked the principal to call 911. It was later learned that his mom was only drunk.

One cute little third grade girl wrote in her daily journal about being scared when she was in the car when her baby-sitter robbed a bank. She included all of the details; waiting in the car, speeding across the railroad tracks, hiding in the back seat when the police went by, and helping count the money. The police were notified and a crime was solved, but nothing could be done to erase that terrible memory. Is it any wonder that teachers shed many tears?

Get Up-close and Personal—Many diseases are caused by viruses which are passed from one person to another person who is in close contact. One way to be sure to never catch these diseases is to never allow other people to get close to you. In the same way, many of the heartaches that we experience in our lives are caused by sharing the trials, tribulations, and traumas of those persons whom we love and are close to. We could totally avoid this by not getting involved and living our lives in such a way that we never allow ourselves to develop close relationships with other people. The more blessed we are by having the opportunity to make a difference in the lives of young people, and having close friends and family, the more vulnerable we become to the threat of disease and heartache. Those of us who choose to serve in the education profession are thus blessed and will inevitably suffer as those we care about have problems and eventually die. That is the price we must pay but this is better than to never experience joy and love in our lives. The way to never be criticized or suffer distress is to do nothing and not get involved.

Goodwill Accounts—Why should we care? Why get involved? We don't owe it to them—or do we?

Everybody knows that they are in trouble when they receive a notice from the bank showing that they have spent more money than they have put in. Our financial bank account must balance. I preached to kids for years that the same thing is true in regard to our "Goodwill Accounts."

It is a good practice to call kids who do well in school to the principal's office to congratulate them. They can then be told that the principal would be honored if some day they included his name on a list of references. He can tell them that a good way to live their life is to look upon it as an opportunity to accumulate as many persons as possible who they feel confident would write a positive reference for them some day when they might need it. In other words, live your life in such a manner that you keep a healthy balance on the plus side in your goodwill account.

Most of us were blessed as kids to have been the recipient of a flood of goodwill from family, neighbors, teachers, and church members. This was great then, and we should be thankful we were so fortunate, but it has added to our goodwill account imbalance. This is great motivation to get busy paying back! Most of us can only hope we live long enough to come close to balancing out our goodwill accounts. Little do the recipients of our goodwill know that they are helping us repay a long standing debt. We're stuck with a negative balance in our goodwill accounts and feel the need to even things up.

Back in my teenage years, roughly during the late 1940s and early 1950s, I had only three means of transportation available to me—I could walk, I could ride the bus, or I could hitch-hike. I hitch-hiked around town, back and forth to college, and even to church camp. During WWII, men in the military depended almost exclusively on this method of travel. I accumulated a huge debt of gratitude to the many helpful drivers who gave me rides. I vowed to someday repay that debt by picking up every hitch-hiker I came upon when I grew up and drove a car. This worked only a few years until laws were made against hitch-hiking and those who did hitch-hike became so violent that it was unsafe to pick one up. This has left me with an unpaid debt that I feel an obligation to repay in some other way. I guess that is why Myra and I take a group of elderly ladies shopping every week in the church van and deliver Meals-On-Wheels.

Tar Strips—Eunice is a 93-year-old female who prides herself on attending church services every week in spite of failing health. A nurse helps Eunice out of the car at the curb about 10 yards away from the entrance to the church. Two large male ushers, one on each side of her, help her start walking. Her feet start slowly shuffling with very short steps never leaving the concrete. Her steps gradually speed up and Eunice seems to be making progress. Suddenly she stops. Neither one of the church ushers can see any reason for stopping. Then they notice a tar strip in a crack in the concrete that rises only about a fourth of an inch above the surface. Eunice sees the tar strip as a major obstacle and succeeds in stepping over it only with considerable help from both ushers.

All of us have tar strips in our lives. We perceive some physical, psychological, or social obstacle as major even though others may hardly notice it. A "tar strip" is defined as any obstacle that is, or is perceived by others as being very minimal or totally unnoticed but is seen by the individual in question as major in nature.

We must be alert to others' tar strips. Some task that seems simple to us could be perceived by another person as impossible and cause severe stress. The most important ideas which affect people's behavior are those ideas they have about themselves.

The Inspector—Every morning my wife and I work together to make the bed. We are always sure to puff up the pillows just right and tuck in the sheet down on the bottom end of the bed in a manner that should satisfy even the most particular Navy inspectors that I experienced back in the '50s. I started to wonder why we do that and all of the other "getting ready for inspection" type things. After all, nobody comes into our private bedroom but us. I've come to the conclusion that there resides within each of us an "Inspector." In reality we don't need to satisfy anybody but ourselves. We are even more particular when we get ready for company to visit. Even on those occasions we are our own worst critics. Although sometimes we probably cause ourselves to do things that are not totally necessary, the "Inspector" in us does keep us from becoming slobs.

Principal's Harvest Time

For many a year, I worked in the schools;
shared joys and tears, and enforced all the rules.
I promoted student learning, they knew where I stood;
I kept the fire burning, but did I do any good?

Success can't be judged only by test and by grade;
many years later you'll learn if a difference you've made.
When I meet an adult and hear all that he's done;
that is when I evaluate whether I've lost or have won.

Youthful exuberance causes behavior that's strange;
class clowns and bullies, I've dealt with the entire range.
But a responsible adult eventually evolves from that kid;
who remembers and regrets some of the things that he did.

Optimists, Rotarians—community leaders they become,
could that be the kid who in kindergarten sucked his thumb?
The important thing in evaluating educational results,
is what kind of person kids become as adults.

With the passage of time the Big Picture becomes clear,
The kids that I helped the most were filled with confusion and fear;
The popular rich kids with parents needed me less,
Both types have turned their lives around and experienced success.

The real satisfaction is in playing a small part;
in producing successful adults with both intellect and heart.
To harvest and reap, educators must be patient and wait,
Yes, all the effort was worth it, I can now emphatically state.

Chapter Four
Tall Tales

Getting Our Money's Worth— Those of us who grew up during the Great Depression never leave any uneaten food on our plate. As children, we were conditioned to believe that some poor Chinese child was hungry and that we should do our part to help out by not wasting food. We expect that some day an old Chinese gentleman will thank us for saving his life when he was young. When we go to an all-you-can-eat-for-one-price buffet, we eat far more than we should. We subconsciously feel that it is wrong to waste food, and that getting our money's worth is not only the patriotic thing to do, but it will make our parents proud of us. This same *get your money's worth even if it kills you* mindset sometimes carries over into other areas of our lives. When we finally throw away washcloths, they can correctly be called "washrags." Bars of soap look like small chips of wood before we use a new bar. When we attend athletic contests, we always stay until the game is over and both teams leave the field, no matter how bad the weather or what the score might be. I found a bright orange colored shirt at the store marked 75% off. My wife suggested that I should not buy it because "It isn't your style." I replied, "To save money, I can change my style."

Once, we attended a music program in Nashville. We had never heard of any of the performers or the songs they sang. We went to the program with the expectation that we would hear some good old songs that would bring back pleasant memories. Instead, most of the singers started their introduction by saying, "Here's a song I wrote last night." The program lasted four hours. We stayed until the bitter end. We noticed that lots of people were leaving between songs. When the lights finally went on there were only about a half-dozen people left in the audience; all depression babies like us. I didn't hear much that went on. After the show someone told me that they announced at the beginning that amplifiers were available for those with hearing problems, but I didn't hear the announcement. The next day we went to an amusement park. The daily admission price covered riding on all the rides and attending all of the shows. We attended every show, rode on the merry-go-round, got sopping wet riding on a floating log version of a roller coaster, and took a beating on the bumper cars. We had a great time and were exhausted at the end of the day. We were determined to get our money's worth even if it almost killed us.

No matter where we go or what show we attend, it seems that the same guy with a big head or hairdo follows us and sits directly in front of us. He even stands up in front of us at football games and takes up space in front of doors and in crowded hallways. He disguises himself to look different, but I'm convinced that it must be the same "Big Head." He obviously has no idea that he is in our way!

I sat in my hot car for thirteen minutes one day, waiting for the time to run out on the parking meter so I would get my money's worth out of it … and I once drove around town to put miles on my car because I hadn't quite used up all of my miles before an oil change was recommended.

The Irish Poet—I saw in the newspaper that a "well-known Irish poet," whom I had never heard of, would read his poetry at our local university. The performance was free, and I had nothing else to do, so I attended. Much to my surprise, about 150 other people did the same thing. Usually, when I go to athletic contests I can count on running into lots of friends. On this occasion I found myself out of my comfort zone and circle of acquaintances. I looked around and didn't recognize a soul. It was as if I was at some fancy country club to which I didn't belong. The poet started reading and I realized that I could only understand about half of his words. I couldn't understand because of the combination of my poor hearing, the poet's strong Irish accent, and a flow of seemingly meaningless and unrelated words. To make matters worse, he read one of his poems in Russian. I thought he was talking about his cow, but found out later the poem was about his car. I know that poems don't always need to rhyme, but in this case nothing he read all evening rhymed. The crowd clapped enthusiastically at the end of each poem and I noticed a condescending, know-it-all smile on most of their faces. Most of the men had long hair, well groomed beards, and thick eyebrows. Some of the women were dressed like men. Everyone was playing the role of aristocratic academic to the hilt. I thought, "What a charade, you can't fool me, you don't understand what the guy says any more than I do!" I couldn't leave because I was seated right in the middle of the room. My only hope was that the poet would need to go to the bathroom because of all of the water he was drinking to keep his throat from drying up. Finally, the ordeal was over.

Feet Hymns— Last Sunday, we sang two of my favorite feet hymns. I always have to chuckle a little when I sing *Take my feet and let them be, swift and beautiful for thee*, and *Oh be swift my soul to answer him, be jubilant my feet*. The idea of my feet being considered swift and beautiful, or jubilant, doesn't match the condition in which I usually find them. Oh, how great it would be to have jubilant and swift feet! Maybe I had them at one time in my life, but it was a long time ago. Since I've retired I have the time to cut my toenails regularly and otherwise upgrade the condition of my feet. But jubilant or swift? No way!

We attended the rendition of Handel's Messiah on Palm Sunday. I was impressed by the text of one of the soprano's solos. It is taken from Romans 10:15 and goes this way: "How beautiful are the feet of them that preach the gospel of peace, and bring glad tidings of good things." I am now attempting to do this and hope it makes my feet beautiful.

Trumpet Playing in Church— One of my bench buddies said that his son-in-law complained about the loud trumpet playing at church. He said, "Every time I go to church they play a trumpet!" My bench buddy responded, "They only play it on Christmas and Easter."

Peanut Season— A small Catholic church in Western Kansas has added a new twist to the seasons of the church year. They have added *Peanut Season* to the calendar. The building has a wooden floor. The trustees of the church decided that the best way to keep it well polished is to place several bushels of peanuts in the entry way and ask the parishioners to eat peanuts during the services and throw the shells on the floor. They then walk on the shells during the month long peanut season. The floor shines brightly when the shells are finally swept off.

Helpful Drunk— I met one of my old high school buddies. He had recently retired after serving as Chief of Police for over 25 years. He told me about an incident that happened back when he was a rookie cop. A lady had locked her keys inside of her car and he was busy using a wire attempting to get her driver's side door open. A well known drunk staggered down the street and tried to get his attention. My buddy told him he didn't have time to mess with him, to be quiet, to mind his own business, and leave. Finally, after he got the driver's side door open, he reluctantly said to the drunk, "OK, now what do you want?" The drunk replied smugly, "I was only trying to tell you that the window is open on the passenger's side."

Cody—Cody was a large, black Labrador retriever. Officially, he lived down the street about two blocks from our house. In reality and unofficially, he was the entire neighborhood's pet. He was strong and hearty; definitely an outdoor type dog, but had the gentle disposition of a sweet child. He ambled along from one house to another, never in a hurry, making friendly house calls. Everybody loved him as though he was their own dog. Kids played with him; men talked to him like an old friend, and women saved bones and other culinary delights for him. Sometimes he smelled musty and wet, other times he had a slight skunk smell to him; but he always acted like a complete gentleman. At times he appeared to be smiling and you could tell when he said, "Hello," and "Thank You."

Some new neighbors move in and poured a new concrete driveway. They observed Cody walking across the new cement and leaving his paw prints. They shot a pellet gun at him and demanded that the county animal control officer pick him up. Fortunately, the animal control officer knew Cody and served as a mediator to save him from the disgrace of being locked up in the animal shelter. The entire neighborhood came to Cody's defense. It was as if someone had attacked a member of the family. The new neighbors quickly got the message and soon were just as fond of Cody as everyone else. One day Cody quit making his rounds. We never did find out the details of his death, but we all felt like we had lost a close friend. The kids say that he is up in heaven with the angels and will be the first to greet us when we get there.

Pledge of Allegiance—The Optimist Club meets weekly at a local Chinese restaurant. They were preparing to open the meeting by reciting the Pledge of Allegiance when they noticed that the American Flag was missing. One of the members joked that they might be forced to use the Chinese flag. The club president looked down the hallway and saw a beer delivery man with an American flag on his uniform. They had the delivery man stand up in front of the room while they all faced him and recited the pledge. When it was over the beer man bowed deeply, tipped his hat and left.

That story reminded me of the opening ceremony of the tractor-pull event at the Vinland Fair. The announcer asked everyone to take off their hats and face a small flag which had been tied to a light pole. An old tape recording of the National Anthem was then played over an old antique public address system. It sounded like it came from the bottom of a barrel. About half way through the tape started to drag, and then it stopped altogether. The announcer reluctantly said, "Well, that's good enough. Gentlemen start your engines!" Two hundred tractor engines roared in unison. That is America at its best!

National Anthem— The band started to play our National Anthem and everyone, except two older men, stood up immediately and removed their hats to show respect. I noticed this and thought how disrespectful these two guys were. I am a Navy veteran and I have spent a lifetime teaching kids to show respect for our country. I was determined to say something to them when the band quit playing. About half-way through the anthem, they finally struggled slowly to their feet. A little bit later, they removed their hats. It was then that I noticed that they were very seriously physically handicapped and had a patch on their hats that said, "Disabled Veteran." They could stand erect only with considerable effort and pain. I talked to them and learned that they had served in combat during W.W.II in Europe and each of them had lost an arm and a leg. I judged too quickly!

Lost Tooth— My first grade granddaughter lost one of her front teeth at school. The tooth came out while she was out in the hallway and she literally lost it. She was extremely upset because she thought she needed it to put under her pillow for the tooth fairy. Grandma came to the rescue by providing a tooth from a jar where she had kept the teeth of our own children when they had lost their teeth. The antique tooth saved the day! The tooth fairy leaves more money now than when I was a kid!

Cousin Glenn—Glenn was given a VCR machine for Christmas. His goal was to get it programmed before the one year warranty ran out. He finally thought he had succeeded, only to discover that he had AM and PM mixed up. It blinked on for another year.

He said that he played softball and basketball until he had to give them both up because his eyes went bad and he couldn't see the ball. Then he became an umpire!

He overheard a farmer in the mall say to his grandson, "Why do you want me to spend a quarter so you can ride one of those fake horses when we have five real ones at home?"

He thought he might buy a large shiny metal tool container for the back of his pickup truck. That way when he dies his descendants could take the tools out of it and he could be buried in it.

He grew up during the 1930s and 1940s in a rural home with no electricity. When he entered the Navy during WWII, they gave him a test and determined that he was best suited to be an Electrician's Mate. He said that his family didn't know that the Japanese had bombed Pearl Harbor until three days later. Their neighbor had a battery powered radio and they liked to listen to Joe Lewis' boxing matches. He and his brother hurried to finish milking the cows and ran down to the neighbors only to be told, as they approached the house, that Joe Lewis had knocked out his German opponent in the first round.

Cheap Fun— On Tuesdays we can go to a movie that normally costs $1.75 for only fifty cents. Being the penny pincher that I am, I go often, even if the movie being shown is no good. After my eyes have adjusted to the dark, it is fun to sit and watch the people come in and stagger and feel around like they are blind and yell to their family, "Where are you?" I would like to grab them on the shoulder and yell, "Boo" and see what they do. My buddy told me that when he went to a movie when was a kid he only had a dime to spend on refreshments. After doing a comprehensive study, he determined that the best way to get the most for his money was to buy a package of licorice flavored Smith Brothers Cough Drops.

Hearing Aid—The hearing aid for my right ear quit working, so I took it in for maintenance. The local representative was not able to fix it, so it had to be sent back to the factory. All I could hear for two weeks was from the left, and I noticed that I was becoming more and more liberal. That's what happens when you only listen to the left.

Organ Music— A good friend of mine was vacationing in downtown London, England when he heard beautiful organ music coming from inside of a church. He thought that the organist must be practicing and, because he was a church organist himself and loved organ music, he decided to go into the church and listen. He entered the back of the church and sat down in a pew. Soon others joined him and he realized that he was attending a funeral! The way out was now blocked by mourners, so he had no choice but to stay until the service was over. As he was leaving, a fellow mourner said to him, "How well did you know the deceased?" He replied, "Not as well as I wish I had."

Serious Problems— As a member of the "Greatest Generation," I survived a World War, The Great Depression, and 38 years in public schools, most of it as a Jr. High principal. After all that, it is hard for some unenlightened people to believe that I could now be complaining and writing letters to the editor about what they consider trivial issues. I wrote a letter because it really bothers me that the newspaper puts the obituaries, comics, and the crossword puzzle in the same section. I want to read the obituaries and the comics first thing in the morning, only to find out that my wife is working the crossword puzzles in that same section. Another thing that I mentioned in my letter is that most of the restaurants stop serving breakfast at 10:30 AM. It is almost impossible to get there that early. I thought that newspapers and restaurants really wanted advice and input, but I haven't seen any changes.

Organ Recitals—We use our church van to take a group of elderly ladies shopping once a week. Much of the talk during the van trips is about health issues. They complain about their hearts, kidneys, lungs, livers, and every other organ in the human body. We call these trips, "Organ Recitals."

One of the ladies joked (I think she was joking) that she doesn't see how farmers can keep track of the various kinds of chickens running around the farmyard—extra crispy, hot and spicy, original recipe, roasted, sweet and spicy—and what in the world would a boneless chicken look like!!?? She said that her grandson visits her often and always asks for green beans for dessert instead of the ice cream that she tries to give him.

Another lady said that her doctor told her that she has high blood pressure. He recommended that she buy a home blood pressure monitoring kit. She bought one but took it back to the store the following day because, "My blood pressure registered too high on it and also the second half of the directions on how to use it were written in Spanish." Another lady told me that she bought a radio and had the same problem—half of the directions were written in Spanish. She returned it to the store because she worried that half of the news on that radio might be in Spanish and she wouldn't be able to understand it.

Hand Count— The 2000 presidential election was "too close to call." The Democrats demanded a "hand count" of the ballots in Florida. I thought it would be funny to pretend that I thought that meant to have everyone for one of the candidates hold up their hand while someone counted hands. I pointed out that it would be harder to count hands, because they would be moving, than to count ballots. Nobody thought my comment was funny. Maybe just have everyone for one of the candidates yell, "Yes" or "No."

Drive-Through—I observed a lady sitting in her car in the drive-through lane at a restaurant yelling her order into a trash can. When she got no response, she yelled even louder. Finally, she muttered something about poor service, and drove off.

Memorial Urinal— I used the men's restroom during the intermission of the College Easter presentation of "The Messiah." I was surprised to see an official looking framed sign posted above one of the urinals that read, *"Dr. Willard Engstrand Memorial Urinal."* My first thought was that this might be a nice and fitting way to remember a valued member of the college faculty who had died, but possibly a little strange! When I left the building I noticed that Dr. Willard Engstrand was currently listed as one of the professors of chemistry. I laughed and considered this a harmless and humorous joke, only to find out later that it wasn't so funny to the college administration. They didn't think it was funny when some creative student replaced the liquid soap in the gymnasium bathroom with beer either—and neither did I! I guess it is a little different when you are directly involved.

Baseball Hall-of-Fame— I went on a trip to visit the baseball Hall-Of-Fame with my son, son-in-law, and a group of their friends. We flew from Kansas City to Syracuse, New York. When we exited the plane I noticed that a large crowd had gathered around a midget. They were staring at him and making a big fuss about him. My first thought was how cruel and uncaring the group was to draw attention to the midget and make fun of him. Then one of my traveling companions explained to me that the guy was a famous movie star and was giving out autographs. I hadn't ever seen him on television because I tend to watch different shows than younger people. He enjoyed the attention and was a great person. I guess wearing sunglasses to cover up his identity, like many celebrities do, wouldn't work very well for him. Sometimes first impressions are not accurate. I got his autograph and made a new friend.

One old lady told me that she was inducted into her high school's Sports Hall-Of-Fame because she had devoted 24 years of her life to being a ticket taker at football games. I've attended games longer than that—maybe I could get in.

Teaching Swimming— When I was a teacher, I divided my time during the summer between going to graduate school and working as a swimming pool manager, swimming instructor, and lifeguard. A crowd of mothers usually gathered along the fence when I taught swimming lessons to their kids. Once when I was demonstrating how to do a prone glide, I pushed off the side of the pool very vigorously and my swimming suit slid down around my ankles. I heard a large roar of laughter but had no other choice but to come up out of the water with a red face and proceed with the instruction. Several mothers who were watching told me later that the buns of my rear end were very white when contrasted with the dark tan of the rest of my body. One of the first things I always taught adult females to do was to float on their backs. This seems to be easy for ladies because they have lots of body fat, which helps them float, and because they don't need to put their face in the water. I explained that it helped to stretch their hands high above their head, with their palms facing up and under the water, and arch their back as much as possible. Then the unexpected happened! I looked around, and all of the ladies were lying on their backs in the water with the front of their one-piece swimming suits pulled down. Each lady had two bare breasts sticking straight up out of the water. They looked like a dozen pairs of huge bobbers, waiting for the fish to bite. None of them noticed it because they were looking straight up at the sky and were concentrating on arching their backs and keeping their lungs full of air. Finally I blew my whistle to end the activity. We practiced the back float every day.

Cold Weather—One of my bench buddies told me about going deer hunting with his friend on a cold, snowy, winter day. His partner experienced success early in the day and agreed to wait in the truck to give him a chance to bag a deer. After waiting in the truck for about an hour, he felt a drastic need to go to the bathroom. He had been experiencing diarrhea for about a week. He walked a short distance from the truck and off of the road several yards. He pulled his bib overalls and the sweat suit under it down around his feet and squatted to do his job. He pulled his sweat suit and overalls up when he had completed his task. It was bitter cold so he pulled the hood on his sweat suit up over his head. Then disaster struck! He had filled his hood with wet slimy fecal matter and now it was all over his head and dripping down over the rest of his body. The next hour was the most miserable of his life. It was too cold to take all of his smelly clothes off. Sitting in the truck with the heater on was very unpleasant. He wanted to head for home but he couldn't find his hunting partner. We all thought it was funny when he told us about it but he never saw any humor in the incident. It reminded him of the time when he didn't have any toilet paper available so he wiped with what turned out to be poison ivy. The worst part of that incident was explaining to the pretty young nurse at the hospital how poison ivy came in contact with his bare rear end.

Another sad memory connected with his hunting hobby was the time when he found a dead blackbird. He thought it might have died from the West Nile Virus, so he put it in a plastic bag and into the freezer so he could turn it in to the county health department the next day. His wife cooked it for supper.

One of my buddies attended a football game at Soldier Field in Chicago on one of the coldest days of the year. He was all bundled up with multiple layers of clothing, which was covered by a one piece fur-lined snowsuit. He went to the concession stand to buy some liquid refreshments. He walked down what seemed like hundreds of steps to get to the concession stand. After missing the entire first quarter of the game standing in line, he purchased four cups of drinks. He was doing his best to carry these with his hands covered with mittens and his cheeks turning blue from the cold. Stepping up a step was almost impossible because all of the extra pants he had on functioned as a splint and he couldn't bend his knees. Then the worst happened! He slipped and fell, spilling the contents of all four of the cups on people sitting next to the aisle. They yelled some very uncomplimentary comments at him. He wanted to just get back to his seat but he couldn't get up because his snowsuit had the effect of a straight jacket and he couldn't bend. Then two nice policemen rescued him. He knew, and the policemen knew, that he was only being helped to his seat, but the crowd assumed that he was being kicked out of the game and commenced to boo the policemen. His buddies finally came to his rescue. He never went to another football game at Soldier Field.

Weather Report—What I don't understand is why any product would sponsor the weather report on television. When the weather is terrible and weatherman says, "Today's weather is brought to you by product X," why would anyone buy product X? After all, product X is bringing us terrible weather. Another question that I wonder about is how the weather knows to do as the weather man tells it to do and stay on a certain side of a particular highway? And how did the weather know where to go before highways were built?

Vests—A new *Cabela's Outdoor Store* opened in Kansas City. I was wandering around in the store when I spied a sign that said, "Insulated Vests $15." I tried on several, making sure to pick out size extra-large. I was surprised that none of them fit me. Then I looked at the sign again and realized they were dog vests. No wonder none of them fit! I had a good laugh and then looked around to see if anyone had observed my stupidity. Fortunately, I was alone.

Drinking Water—Our friends recently moved from Salina to Lindsborg. The family adjusted well, but their large Labrador dog got sick and refused to drink water. Quite by accident, they discovered that he didn't like the taste of Lindsborg water. When he drank the water it made him sick. Everyone in the family drank regular tap water, but they had to purchase bottled water for the dog.

Band Concerts—We love to attend summer band concerts in the park. On one occasion, an elderly man, who appeared to have lost some of his mental sharpness, sat in a lawn chair in the front row and clapped vigorously to the beat of the music. He made wide sweeping motions with his arms and his timing was way off. The band members became so distracted that in the middle of a musical number he became the conductor. The music sounded very "different."

Clean Dirt—I saw a sign that read, "Clean Dirt For Sale." For the next 30 minutes I analyzed in my mind the concept of "Clean Dirt." I wondered if you were covered with this, would you be considered clean or dirty? "Clean" always has been the opposite of "Dirty" in my mind and "Dirty" meant dirt.

Birthday Celebrations and False Teeth— One of my bench buddies celebrated his birthday a little too much and ended the evening vomiting in the toilet. In the process, he cut his forehead when the toilet seat fell down on him. He also lost his false teeth. The whole incident didn't set too well with his wife. He put some *Udder Balm* on the cut to help it heal. I had always thought that *Udder Balm* was the name of a German super highway but found out that it is a salve that works wonders on the underside of cows. False teeth are too expensive to just go buy another set, so he decided that his best bet would be to spend the next day pumping out his septic tank. He hoped that if he got all of the liquid out of it, he could fish his false teeth off of the bottom of the tank. Word got out around town what was going on. It wasn't long before most of the population of the town was taking turns peering into his septic tank and making rude comments. When the tank was finally empty, the elusive teeth were still not to be found. He then unbolted the toilet from the floor and had me help him carry it out in his backyard where the two of us shook the devil out of it. Finally the false teeth fell out and we had reason to celebrate all over again. The next day everyone asked him if they could smell his breath. He suggested that the two of us could share the same set of teeth. That isn't practical because I have a partial plate on the bottom and my buddy's is on the top. It never hurts to explore alternatives.

Cosmopolitan Guy—Our local business community sponsors an annual "Huff and Puff" hot air balloon rally. A large poster advertising the event hung on the wall of the grocery store over a bench. I thought it would be funny to have my buddy Bernie sit directly under the large word "Huff" and me under "Puff" and have our picture taken. Much to my dismay, before I could arrange to get the history making picture taken, the sign was replaced by a sign advertising a $99.99 Grandfather clock. The clock was made in China. You wouldn't think there would be much demand for a clock made by a Chinese grandfather, with Roman numerals. I checked my clothing and discovered that everything I wore was made in some other country, except my underwear. But a Chinese grandfather clock makes no sense.

Although I have spent the vast majority of my life in Kansas, I feel like I qualify as a cosmopolitan guy. My shoes were made in China; my hats and pants were made in Mexico; my socks were made in Germany; and my shirts were made in Honduras, India, and a place that I have never heard of called Mauritius. This should qualify me as a man of the world. They say, "Clothes make the man."

My buddy said that his left shoe was made in China and his right one was made in Mexico. They are the same brand, style, and size, but one was a little bit darker color than the other. I asked him if there wasn't a difference in the size of a Chinese man's foot and that of a Mexican man. I would think that would cause a problem. I would think his feet might get confused about which direction to go because of the difference in language. Wouldn't a "Medium" shirt in Japan be smaller than a "Medium" shirt in Sweden?

Virtually—I saw a sign advertising "Virtually New Clothing." I wondered how that could be, so I looked the word "Virtually" up in the dictionary. It means, "In effect, although not in fact," or "For all practical purposes." Using this concept, I am promoting "Virtually Handicapped" parking permits. I have always wanted to have the advantage of parking in "Handicapped" parking stalls. I even joked that I would give an arm and a leg to be handicapped. Now I can claim that I am "Virtually Handicapped."

Knee Pads—I just returned from an appointment with my doctor. I told him, "I don't care what kind of pills you prescribe for me, just so they are not the same color as the linoleum on the floor of my bathroom." I always drop pills and can't find them because they blend in with the colors of the floor. Once, I experienced pain on the bottom of one of my feet and discovered that the cause was a pill that had stuck to the bottom of my foot. One Tuesday morning I dropped my weekly pill organizer on the bathroom floor and all of the pills for the rest of the week flew all over. The night before I had reached for a Vick's container and it rolled off of the bed stand and down onto the bedroom floor. I didn't want to wake up my wife so I crawled around on the floor, groping and feeling my way around in the dark, until I finally gave up. One day my wife opened the door while I was crawling around in the bathroom looking for a pill. The door hit me on the head and it almost knocked me out. When I finally stood up I felt so miserable that I needed to double the dose. I bet my grandkids will be surprised when I ask for a new set of knee pads for Christmas. I'll just tell them that I am taking up playing volleyball.

Historical Record—In recent years I have learned to appreciate old family pictures, heirlooms, and historical records. One of my former students is the owner of a business that sells and repairs tires. He has collected a jar full of objects that his staff has taken out of tires that caused flats. This inspired me to look for ways to do something similar. I wish now that over the years when I cleaned my whisker clippings out of my electric razor I had put them into a clear glass container. The whiskers in the bottom of the container would be darker. They would represent my younger years. The clippings would gradually get grayer as the years pass. Those on the top would be almost white. I could have called it my "Pepper and Salt" collection. Labels on the outside of the glass could have documented the progressive years. We did a similar thing by marking the height of our kids on a door, with a date next to each mark, as they grew up. It might have been good to also include hair clippings after haircuts, and even finger and toenail clippings. When I was but a young lad of eight, I gained much of my worldly knowledge from older and wiser kids of nine and ten years of age while sitting on the curb down on the corner in the evening. They told me that when a person is dead, his hair, whiskers, and finger nails keep on growing. I guess there would be no practical way to top off the collection with these.

I suggested to my grandson that he start such a collection. He listened politely, shrugged his shoulders, made a grimacing face, and said that he didn't see any sense in doing it. He said that he didn't see how it would have been possible for me to do this because electricity probably hadn't been invented yet when

I first started shaving. When he gets older he'll become more sensible and wish he had taken my advice.

Sunday Morning Sounds— During all of the years prior to my retirement I got out of bed immediately when awakened by an alarm clock in the morning. Sunday mornings were different. Our family didn't need to arrive at Sunday School until nine o'clock. That presented the luxurious option of staying in bed longer. I could engage in my favorite non-activity, which I refer to as *lying and listening*. I could hear the precisely timed one long and two short toots of a turtle dove, the distinctive call of the bob-white quail, the rumble and plaintive whistle of a distant train, raindrops falling on the roof, noises from the kitchen made by my dear sweet wife who was busy preparing for the weekly influx of twenty people for Sunday lunch, a woodpecker who sounded as if he was destroying our house, and in the wintertime the sound of a snowplow. I thought to myself, "Wow, life doesn't get any better than this!" But life did get better—when I retired and could enjoy Sunday morning sounds everyday. Money can't buy that kind of happiness, tranquility, and contentment.

Help Needed Listening—I accidentally cut my hand attempting to open a salt shaker. I twisted too hard and the glass broke. Usually, when I cut myself, I just pull the wound shut and use tape to hold it shut until it heals. This cut was deep and on a spot that constantly moves, so I decided to go to the emergency room. After putting six stitches in my hand to hold the wound closed, the doctor, said, "Come back in eight to nine days and have the stitches removed." On the way home I commented that 89 days was a long time to wait before getting stitches out. My wife clarified the situation. It is a good thing she went to the hospital with me.

Golf Courses—I never feel comfortable around country clubs or any other type of golf course. When I was a kid I worked several summers as a caddy at the most exclusive country club in Topeka. To this day, when I am around a golf course, I identify more with the employees than with the members. I expect someone to tap me on the shoulder and say, "Boy, carry my clubs." We had an administrator's party at the country club. It was made clear that I was expected to wear a suit and tie. That was about the only thing that was clear to me about the arrangements. I told Myra that, because we were in such a fancy place and the food and drink prices would be high, to order the lowest priced thing on the menu and only to drink water. We both acted like we really were not hungry and ordered sandwiches for $3.50. When the social affair was over, the lady in charge announced that because no one had kept track of what each of us had eaten we would just divide the bill up evenly. Our share was $22.00 each or a total of $44.00.

Dogs—I was enjoying one beautiful summer evening sitting on my daughter's deck. My only company was her cute little dog named "Roxie." Roxie was entertaining me by chasing her tail and doing other simple tricks. When she looked up at me for approval, I said, "Do you like being a dog?" Then I realized how stupid it is to talk to a dog; and even worse, to ask a dog a question and expect an answer. I shared this experience with a lady during a break in the action at a basketball game. She laughed and then told me that she often talks to herself. She said that one time she even talked to herself in a British accent. I tried doing that but, after all of these years of living in the Midwest, English accents just don't come easy. A retired principal buddy told me, "When I talk to my dog I sometimes use some down home grammar that I don't often use with other family members. The dog won't criticize."

I noticed at a funeral that an old lady had a dog sitting on her lap. The next evening I observed that several couples had brought their dogs to the band concert in the park. I guess I'll ask Roxie if she wants to start attending funerals and band concerts with me.

Dead Animal Remover—The government has developed a very successful program that encourages community groups to "Adopt a Highway." A civic group selects a specific section of a local road on which they pick up trash. I guess that doesn't include road-kill. The bodies of dead animals remain on the roadway for weeks on a two mile portion of highway that I regularly drive. My first reaction was to place blame on governmental agencies. Our Sheriff is my good friend and we visit weekly at Optimist club meetings. When I brought up the subject he thought I was joking and had a good laugh. I guess he thought that I was just once more displaying my goofy sense of humor. He has enough to worry about dealing with human bodies. He suggested that removing dead animals from the roadway would make a good project for a retired school administrator who has nothing better to do. That settled it! I adopted that two mile stretch. I became a self-appointed unofficial "Dead Animal Remover." (DAR) I thought about starting a Kansas Chapter of the DAR, but was told that one already exists. (Daughters of the American Revolution) Since that fateful day, I have removed all kinds of dead animals, in various states of decay, and under a wide variety of weather conditions. It has become a real challenge, and I have actually learned to enjoy the thrill and excitement. It gives me a true sense of accomplishment. I have developed specialized techniques and use different lengths of sticks for squirrels, raccoons, skunks, dogs, and cats. Initially I buried the remains in the ditch, had a short private memorial service, and placed a small white cross on the site. I quit doing that because I was never sure what denomination the animal might be and didn't want to take the chance that I might put a Christian cross on the grave of a Moslem or Buddhist animal. I made the mistake of placing a dead skunk in my car trunk once. (That might make a good title for a book, "A skunk in the trunk") I thought about using the remains to feed poor hungry people, sell it to restaurants, or even sew the pelts together and make a fur coat to give to my wife for Christmas. Each of these concepts had some minor flaw. For example, I couldn't figure out how to remove the tire tracks for the coat project. I might write a scholarly book on the topic. It would probably make the "Best Smeller" list. Former co-workers and students wave at me and laugh. I think some have even tried to run over me! I guess they think that I have finally found my true calling. Early in my new career I suffered severe shock every time that a carcass moved. I now know that movement can be caused by a gust of wind. A retired principal buddy told me, "I would think a principal would be better suited for cleaning out stables or barn lots. I know I shoveled a lot of manure in my day—threw some, too. Do you qualify for a government subsidy? Seems to me you are helping the clean air situation." I shared these deep concepts with my buddy Bernie. He reminded me of all of the conversations we have had in the past over coffee about how sad it is to waste all of the dogs that are put to sleep, when some of the poorest and hungriest people in the world would happily eat them.

Rest Home Visit—My former vice-principal died from complications of Alzheimer's disease. When he was in the early stage of the disease I picked him up in my truck and we went walking at the mall. One day his wife gave him a banana to take along to eat if he got hungry. He pealed the banana and matter-of-factly put the peel in my glove box. Later, when he was in a rest home, I would take him for walks down the hall. One day we sat down on chairs to rest and were soon joined by about ten other patients. Little did I know that we had accidentally dropped into a therapy session for patients whose disease had not advanced as much as my friend's. A pretty young therapist went around the circle and asked each of us to name one of Santa's reindeer. She came to me and yelled in my face, "Name one of Santa's reindeer." I yelled back, "Rudolph." She patted me on the head and said, "Good Boy." On another occasion I took him outside to a fenced-in play area. The management accidentally locked us in there and I had to climb over a fence to get out. Every time I visited him I was asked by a pathetic old lady in a wheelchair to push her. I asked her "Where are you going?" She replied "I don't know." She just wanted to go for a ride; and why not? An old man sitting on the porch commented, "This weather is terrible, not like we used to have!" One day, when the weather was nice, he said, "It's a good day to be above ground." I noticed that it is almost impossible to get a standing ovation in a rest home. Most of the patients can't stand up.

I Wonder! I don't know which is worse, (1) Having to wait while the slow-witted old man in the car ahead of me gets around to going when the red light changes to green, or (2) Listening to the young smart aleck in the car behind me honk when I don't get started fast enough to suit him.

I also wonder why a person would bother to call in to the television opinion poll, or go to the trouble of looking up and responding to a computer web site, to say that they have no opinion.

The Homecoming Queen of Forty-Nine

The Homecoming Queen of forty-nine,
So clean and fresh, she looked so fine.
All admired her when she wore the crown,
Much sought after, she was the "toast of the town."
But the passing years have been unkind,
For now she's wrinkled in spirit, body, and mind.
She shuffles through the streets carrying a yellow "Dollar Store" sack,
With sore aching feet and a throbbing hump on her back.
So many poor choices she made along the way!
For life is more serious than the senior play.
She wed her first husband because in high school he had muscles,
And got cheers on the athletic field for his jumping and hustles.
Though strong in body, he was weak in his mind,
He hit her, abused her, and never treated her kind.
The second she married because he had lots of money,
But he was mean in spirit and never called her "Honey."
The third she chose because of his handsome looks,
But soon she discovered he couldn't even read books.
Too late she learned that skills that look huge in high school,
Don't count for much years later, she had been such a fool.
So now to console herself lots of alcohol she drinks,
Of tobacco and garbage and body odor she stinks.
Don't make the same mistake and ruin your dream,
Marry the articulate, smart captain of the Forensic and Debate team.

What Is "Quality of Life" for a Turtle? And for an Old Man?

(An actual experience of the author)

The old man sat in his yard, in a comfortable chair,
His eyes locked straight ahead, in a glassy stare,
His mind gradually awoke, as he sat there alone,
Like a slight puff of gray smoke, was what he saw a smooth stone?
Then smiling in surprise, he observed a long neck,
And a head with beady eyes, it's a turtle by heck!
The critter looked as if rejected, as it crawled slowly around,
As if it hoped to be respected, noticed and found.
There seemed to be no logic to his random movement,
He didn't seem to be seeking progress or improvement.
The old man then pondered, "What do turtles do?
His time just seems squandered, and that is true of me too!"
The old man to that turtle himself compared,
Both seemed to have no purpose, it almost made him scared.
Is this what happens, when a young man gets old?
Like that turtle, no purpose, no goals, just exist like mold?
Do turtles feel happiness, contentment and have a "quality of life?"
Or do they only physically survive and attempt to avoid strife?
Is that turtle only aware of things that are currently real?
With no memories or keepsakes—no emotions to feel!
Is physical comfort a turtle's only goal?
Or do they, like us, seek contentment deep in their soul?
Maybe too many people, like that turtle do live,
With no concern about justice, peace, or what they can give.
Then back in his trance, the old man did go,
The answer to these questions he unfortunately never will know.

Printed in the United States
55380LVS00002B/298-330

The stories recorded here are the result of a long career as a building level public school administrator in the educational trenches, time devoted to sharing stories since retirement with fellow "Bench Buddies" on community benches, and drinking coffee and visiting with long-time friends. They include dry humor, tall-tales, and down-to-earth educational philosophy. The author's interests are not terribly academic. The commonplace and daily aspects of life attract him most. Events and stories were recorded over a period of time and consolidated upon retirement.

He has written the following from his perspective as a principal, husband, father, grandfather, community activist, and educator. It reflects his personal philosophy, opinions, sense of humor, and point of view.

Most of what is recorded as fact really did happen but the names have been changed to protect the guilty. Occasional exaggerations can be expected as they make a good story even better.

Charles D. "Chuck" Sodergren, graduated from Bethany College with a BA degree and from Kansas University with a Master of Education degree. He retired in 1995 after working for thirty-eight years in Kansas public schools: five years as teacher; twelve years as elementary principal and twenty-one years as junior high principal.

ISBN 1-4241-4585-6

90000

9 781424 145850

PUBLISH AMERICA

www.PublishAmerica.com